THE MOTHER LODE

Automobile Club of Southern California

COVER PHOTO
St. Xavier Catholic Church, Chinese Camp
by John Austerman

Writer...John Austerman
Artist..Maria E. Morales

Editor...Judy van Wingerden

ISBN: 1-56413-183-1
Printed in the United States of America

Alphabetical List of Contents

GET EVERYTHING FOR YOUR TRIP. FREE.

Maps, TourBooks® & Area Guides

Fee-Free American Express® Travelers Cheques

Car Rental Reservations & Discounts

Complete Airline & Travel Reservations

Hotel/Motel Reservations & Discounts

Join the Auto Club of Southern California today and we'll give you everything you need for your trip. ✦ Free maps ✦ Free TourBooks®, CampBooks® and area guides ✦ Fee-free American Express® Travelers Cheques and ✦ Free Triptiks®, a personalized, mile-by-mile routing of your entire trip. And you'll love saving money with Member-only discounts on ✦ Tours and cruises ✦ Hotel/motel reservations ✦ Rental cars and ✦ Popular attractions across the country. All of these great travel benefits can be yours for $38 a year plus a $20 enrollment fee -- a total of just $58. So why wait? Join AAA today and get everything for your trip. <u>Free</u>!

Call 1-800-882-5550, Ext. 150 (Outside So. CA: 1-800-AAA-HELP)

Dependable Emergency Road Service

Associate memberships for your spouse and children are available for a nominal fee. Membership dues are subject to change without notice.

About This Book

This guidebook focuses on the 267-mile stretch of SR 49 between Mariposa and Sierraville; descriptions of some rewarding side trips are also included. Although Highway 49 extends both north and south of this strip, these areas have little Gold Rush significance. The book traces a tour through the Mother Lode country from south to north, but this does not constitute a recommendation that travelers follow this direction.

The book is divided into three main geographic sections—Southern Mother Lode, Central Mother Lode and Northern Mother Lode—for convenience only. There is neither a natural dividing line between any of these sections nor even a clear-cut agreement as to the boundaries of the Mother Lode itself. Each part contains an introduction to the area covered, along with a strip map showing the routes outlined in the text.

Each section of highway between major communities is described, with special attention to mileage, driving time, road conditions, scenery, roadside facilities and points of interest. Town descriptions are divided into two headings—*Now* and *Then*. Under *Now* the reader will find general information, including population, elevation and a summary of services and facilities. Also contained under the *Now* heading are brief descriptions of points of interest and a notation where AAA discounts are offered. *Then* includes a short history of the area. Descriptions of *Side Trips* are separated from the main copy by a series of diamonds.

The *Alphabetical List of Contents* on page 3 lists towns, personalities and places of historical interest. A glossary defining terms characteristic of the Mother Lode and the Gold Rush appears in the back of the book. It is followed by lists of local chambers of commerce and California State Automobile Association district offices.

Detailed listings of accommodations are available in the AAA *California/Nevada TourBook* and the California State Automobile Association's *Bed and Breakfast* book. Information on camping can be found in the AAA *California CampBook* or the ACSC *Central and Southern California* and *Northern California* camping maps.

The Club also offers detailed road maps of the Mother Lode region. In addition to these publications, the Auto Club provides many other member services designed to make your travels more enjoyable; these include weather and highway information, emergency road services, other maps and publications, reservations and travel insurance.

Introduction

California's Mother Lode country encompasses a narrow belt extending nearly 200 miles along the western slopes of the Sierra Nevada and ranging in elevation from about 700 to over 2500 feet. It is a peaceful, bucolic region characterized by small ranches, quiet little towns and grassy hills dotted with oak and pine. Yet in the mid-19th century, this was the focal point of one of the most frenzied migrations in human history—the California Gold Rush.

Mexican miners coined the term *La Veta Madre* (The Mother Lode), which referred to an incredibly rich vein of gold stretching 120 miles from Bear Valley to Auburn. Later, however, the name "Mother Lode" gradually came to describe the entire gold-rich foothill region from Mariposa to Downieville.

James Marshall's discovery of gold along the American River in 1848 triggered a series of events that propelled California from a remote territory into U.S. statehood. The race for wealth lured thousands of gold-seekers from all parts of the globe, and this once tranquil area erupted with people. Towns were built wherever the yellow metal glinted, then were abandoned when it played out. A valley that was pristine in springtime might have become a mushrooming metropolis in summer, then a ghost town by fall, when the last ounce of gold had been extracted. Or a bustling town might have been torn down by its inhabitants when gold was discovered under its foundations. Of the 546 Mother Lode mining towns described by historians, almost 300 have vanished; some of those that remain are little more than colorful names on a map.

While they lived, the Gold Rush towns existed for only one purpose—to serve the needs of the miners. Wherever the gold-seekers moved, a retinue followed. Saloon keepers came first, often opening for business with nothing more than a plank spanning two barrels. One bartender reported a profit of $7000 on every barrel of whiskey he sold. The ladies of the gold camps appeared next, filling dance halls, gambling dens and the inevitable bawdy houses with the provocative scent of perfume. Then came the merchants, who built stores providing necessities that were only slightly less expensive than the luxuries. A slice of bread cost a dollar, two if it was buttered. A shovel cost $50. Few miners actually became rich; instead, it was those who supplied their needs who grew wealthy.

Life in the gold camps was hard. Health conditions were poor, and there often was no medicine. Lodgings were primitive: most miners lived in tents or crude shelters with walls of canvas, hides or rough-hewn planks. Mining for gold was hard, monotonous labor; it was frequently necessary to stand for hours under a hot sun or in mud or icy water.

The miners probably didn't complain much though, because gold was found virtually everywhere during the early years of the Gold Rush. A man working with just a pan could sometimes glean $10 to $50 per day. One forty-niner found a three-ounce nugget while digging a hole for a tent stake; another discovered a half-pound nugget when he rolled aside a rock he had been using for a seat; still another made a rich gold strike one moonlit night while searching for his lost cow near what was thought to be a mined-out area. A 75-pound nugget was found in Woods Creek, a 141-pound nugget near Sierra City and a 195-pound nugget near Carson Hill. The chance of such instant wealth provided motivation for those who endured the rigors of the gold camps.

In addition to the hardships that awaited miners in California, the journey to the gold fields was long and arduous. According to a popular saying, "The cowards never started, and the weaklings died on the way." Forty-niners had three main choices of travel: a 15,000-mile voyage around Cape Horn; a "shortcut" across the Isthmus of Panama, where malaria, mosquitoes and oppressive heat impeded passage; or a hazardous overland trek across plains and mountains, during which would-be argonauts faced thirst, cholera and unfriendly Indians.

Once they arrived in California, the gold-seekers found the region in turmoil. Mexico had relinquished the reins of government, but the United States had not yet grasped them. Washington was more than 3000 miles away and exerted little influence. Law in the gold fields was usually administered by an *alcalde*—a combination mayor-judge-sheriff who made up laws as were expedient. Where no judiciary existed, miners interrupted their work to form their own system of law, often handing out justice at the end of a rope.

Many of the miners were foreign-born, especially in the southern section of the Mother Lode. But American miners felt they had more right to the gold than the immigrants who swarmed into the fields from other parts of the world. The Americans banished Mexican miners from Quartzburg, chased the Chileans and French from Mokelumne Hill, and drove Chinese miners away from their prosperous diggings. Using their prejudices as justification for their avaricious actions, American miners seized claims for themselves, having little patience for "foreigners."

By 1850, when California achieved statehood, the Mother Lode teemed with gold-hungry men, each of whom was eager to share in the riches. But by the 1860s, placer mining had generally become unprofitable, and many of the miners still remaining in the fields had turned to deep-shaft (quartz) mining, some of them working for large companies. Seeking gold became a business instead of an adventure, as expensive shafts were dug, one to an incline depth of almost 7000 feet. After 1855 giant water hoses called *monitors* had come into use. Entire mountainsides were washed away into muddy streams, which were then sluiced for gold. Valleys became gorged with mud, and portions of San Francisco Bay became clogged with silt. Finally, when legislation brought an end to large-scale hydraulic mining in 1884, the rush for gold came to an end. A few mines continued to operate, but high costs and the fixed price of gold had closed most mines for good by 1942.

7

The Mother Lode Today

Because most of California's phenomenal 20th-century growth and development has taken place in other portions of the state, the gold country has changed more slowly over the years. As a result, the visitor touring the Mother Lode can still recapture a hint of 1849.

Some of the old mining camps, such as Sonora, Placerville, Auburn and Grass Valley, have become busy cities—progressive yet proud of their Gold Rush origins. Others are now tiny rural communities with only a handful of residents. Many buildings from the Gold Rush era still stand, ranging from small adobe huts bearing the Chinese characters of their original inhabitants to substantial structures, such as the Mariposa County Courthouse, built in 1854 and still in use. Others, such as Sutter's Mill at Coloma and Mark Twain's cabin at Jackass Hill, have been rebuilt. The site of Marshall's gold discovery and the Empire Mine near Grass Valley, plus two former boomtowns—Columbia and North Bloomfield—are now preserved in state historic parks. In addition, several museums display fascinating relics of the Gold Rush days.

As impressive as these well-ordered structures may be, many visitors find an even closer link with the past in the deserted mines and dilapidated dwellings scattered throughout the foothills. In most Mother Lode communities there are iron-shuttered buildings, crumbling walls and foundations—reminders of earlier days when the now-peaceful countryside swarmed with gold-hungry miners.

Unfortunately these Gold Rush landmarks become fewer each year as time, fires and "progress" take their toll. Bagby, Jacksonville and Melones now lie under the waters of reservoirs. Grass Valley and Nevada City have lost entire blocks to a freeway, and roads have erased historic Mormon Bar. A trip to the Mother Lode country can be a rewarding step backward in time and offers a fascinating look at California's Gold Rush heritage, but each year there is less to see. Plan to see it before it is too late.

A state highway, appropriately numbered 49, winds through the Mother Lode country. Beginning at Oakhurst in Madera County, State Route 49 climbs and dips through the foothills, then crosses the crest of the Sierra Nevada at Yuba Pass and terminates at Vinton, near the Nevada border. For most of its 325-mile length, SR 49 is a two-lane road. While many sections are wide and mostly level, permitting speeds of up to 55 miles per hour, others are narrow, steep and winding, requiring extra caution from motorists. Congestion is often encountered in major towns. SR 49 remains open all year, but heavy snows occasionally cause temporary closures in the Yuba Pass area.

Although the entire length of SR 49 can be driven in a day or two, most visitors should allow at least five to seven days for an adequate tour of the Mother Lode country. Several interesting destinations lie a few miles off the main highway, and historic landmarks, museums and charming shops all compel attention. Overnight accommodations and restaurants are generally of good quality and sufficient quantity, although they are somewhat limited in the extreme southern and northern portions of the Mother Lode. Campgrounds are most plentiful in the far north. Reservations for accommodations are recommended during summer and on weekends; they are advisable at any time.

Summer is the prime tourist season in the gold country, but it isn't necessarily the most pleasant time of year. Summer days can be hot, accommodations fill up early in the day, and such popular attractions as Columbia and Coloma become quite crowded.

Sutter Creek is one of the most picturesque Mother Lode towns.

Spring—early April through May—is probably the most pleasant season. The weather is comfortably mild, crowds are generally absent, the hills are lush and green, and the countryside is sprinkled with wildflowers. The months of October and November also bring excellent weather and a lack of tourists; fall color can be lovely, especially in the far north.

In 1919 a group of mine operators, merchants and newspaper publishers began an effort to establish a north-south route through the gold country. At the time, a dusty, often impassable trail was the only link between the Mother Lode communities. The route ultimately was added to the state Highway System and designated SR 49 in recognition of the gold rush and the forty-niners.

1994 marks the 75th anniversary of that historic meeting and will be celebrated throughout the Mother Lode during the year, beginning with the highway's rededication of the road and followed by a number of special events. Dates and details of events can be obtained from the Golden Chain Council, P.O. Box 49, Newcastle, CA 95658; (916) 663-2061.

Tom Dell

Mariposa's county courthouse is the oldest in California.

Southern Mother Lode

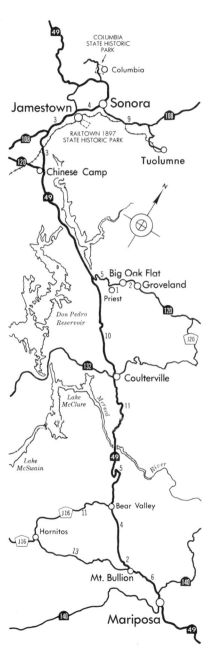

NOW Although busy county seats are located at either end, the southern section is the most sparsely settled portion of the Mother Lode. For the most part, the countryside is decidedly rural in appearance, consisting of rolling hills forested with oak, pine and heavy brush. The climate is somewhat hot and dry in summer but pleasant and mild the rest of the year. Springtime brings colorful wildflower displays. Elevations range from 870 feet at the bottom of the Merced River gorge to about 2200 feet near Mt. Bullion.

THE ROAD For most of its 57-mile length through the southern Mother Lode, SR 49 is a high-speed, two-lane highway with gentle curves and a smooth, wide surface. Where it climbs in and out of the canyon of the Merced River, however, its sharp curves and steep gradient call for reduced speeds and extra caution. The side trips to Hornitos and Groveland are made via steep, somewhat narrow two-lane roads. This section of the Mother Lode is joined at several points by major state highways. For more detailed information, refer to the CSAA *Yosemite* map.

FACILITIES Visitors should plan to make either Mariposa or Sonora their base for touring the southern Mother Lode, since facilities elsewhere are limited. Campgrounds are located several miles off the main highway. See the AAA *California/Nevada TourBook* or the California State Automobile Association's *Bed and Breakfast* book for accommodations listings. For camping information refer to the AAA *CampBook* or the ACSC *Central and Southern* and *Northern California Camping* maps.

RECREATION Yosemite National Park is easily accessible from the southern Mother Lode via either SR 140 or SR 120 (see ACSC's *Guide to Yosemite National Park*). A group of reservoirs located just west of SR 49 offers water sports.

THEN Although gold proved to be less plentiful in the southern section than elsewhere in the Mother Lode, a substantial amount of wealth was accumulated here, and many colorful characters roamed the countryside. Such names as Sonora, Chinese Camp and Mormon Bar recall the diverse population of miners who prospected this area.

11

MARIPOSA

NOW Population 1800; elevation 1953 feet. There are several motels in town and numerous bed and breakfast inns; dining facilities are good but limited in quantity. A wide range of other facilities and services can be found in Mariposa, including a hospital and a small airport.

Mariposa is attractively situated along the slopes and floor of the slender valley formed by Mariposa Creek. SR 49/140 is the town's main thoroughfare; cross streets are steep and narrow. The architecture is a combination of old and new, with many of the earliest buildings having been modernized for business use. Mariposa's economy is sustained by its location along a major highway leading to Yosemite National Park and bolstered by its position as county seat. As the southern gateway to the Mother Lode country, Mariposa takes its heritage seriously and displays many well-kept Gold Rush relics. In March Mariposa holds its popular Storytelling Festival, and on Labor Day weekend, the town hosts the Mariposa County Fair.

California State Mining and Mineral Museum is a mile south of Mariposa on SR 49 at the County Fairgrounds. Housed in a replica of an 1890s mining complex are outstanding exhibits of California gems, minerals, rocks and fossils. The museum also includes a 150-foot-long mine tunnel and scale models of both a fully operational stamp mill and a gold mine's multi-level excavations and intricate tunnels. Among the merchandise offered at the gift and book shop are gemstone jewelry, gold samples and guidebooks to gold-panning sites in the area. The museum is open Wednesday through Monday 10 a.m. to 6 p.m. May through September; Wednesday through Sunday 10 a.m. to 4 p.m. October through April. Adults $3.50; seniors $2.50; ages 13 and under free. (209) 742-7625.

Mariposa County Courthouse, California's oldest, is a white, two-story frame structure built in 1854 at a cost of $9200. Wooden pegs, square nails and hand-planed lumber were used in its construction. The tower clock, installed in 1866, was brought to California by sailing ship around Cape Horn. The courtroom on the second floor contains much of its original furniture. Open 8 a.m. to 5 p.m. Monday through Friday; free conducted tours are given on weekends from Easter week through September. The courthouse is located on Bullion St. between 9th and 10th sts., one block east of the highway. (209) 966-2456.

St. Joseph's Catholic Church, built in 1862, sits on a bluff overlooking SR 49 at the south edge of town. It is a beautiful example of the simple, white, belfry-topped churches found throughout the Mother Lode country.

The Old Jail, located on Bullion St. a few blocks north of St. Joseph's Church, is constructed of blocks of granite and has iron plates and bars over the windows. It was built in 1858 and restored in 1976.

The Mariposa Museum and History Center is just off SR 49 near the north end of town, at 12th and Jessie sts. This combination library and museum contains an exceptional collection of Gold Rush memorabilia, including a five-stamp mill, a monitor nozzle, an Indian village, several horse-drawn vehicles, and replicas of rooms depicting life in the gold camps during the 1850s and 1860s. Also of interest are the counter, interior furnishings and merchandise from the Gagliardo Store

12

Tom Dell

This stamp mill is on display at the Mariposa Museum and History Center.

in nearby Hornitos. Open 10 a.m. to 4:30 p.m. daily, April through October; open 10 a.m. to 4 p.m. weekends only the rest of the year and spring break week; closed in January. (209) 966-2924.

Other points of historical interest in Mariposa: The *I.O.O.F. Hall*, built in 1867 and still used for meetings . . . the *Schlageter Hotel*, with its overhanging balcony, now housing shops and offices . . . the *Masonic Lodge Hall*, on a side street near the I.O.O.F. Hall . . . the *John Trabucco Warehouse*, a Gold Rush-era structure of red brick, with heavy iron doors . . . *Judge Trabucco's home*, a large Victorian residence, located at Jones and 8th sts., east of SR 49 . . . the *Trabucco Building*, constructed of stone and brick. . . . the cemetery, near the northwest edge of town, just off SR 49, with many ornate tombstones . . . some of which date back nearly a century.

13

THEN After gold was discovered here in 1849, Mariposa (Spanish for butterfly) grew within two years from a small cluster of miners' tents into the seat of a 30,000-square-mile county. The leading citizen of early-day Mariposa was Col. John C. Fremont, the famed explorer and army officer. Fremont had purchased a former Mexican land grant of 44,000 acres for $3200 prior to the discovery of gold. After gold was found in nearby placer deposits, Fremont "floated" his holdings, which previously had no set boundaries, to include Mariposa and its rich mines. He imported machinery for the stamp mill, which separated gold from the rich quartz veins uncovered soon after local placer deposits became heavily worked. A company under lease from Fremont laid out the town, naming many of the streets after members of his family. By 1854 Mariposa had acquired its stately courthouse and one of California's first weekly newspapers (still in operation).

But the gold mines eventually closed down. A disastrous fire in the late 1860s wiped out much of the business section, and the town steadily declined. Mariposa County was reduced to its present-day 1455 square miles as other counties annexed most of its territory. Fortunately, discovery of the scenic riches of nearby Yosemite Valley brought a tide of tourists, and the town of Mariposa became an important stopover for travelers.

MARIPOSA TO BEAR VALLEY
(12 miles, 15 minutes)

Beyond Mariposa SR 49 curves gently past fenced grazing lands through rolling countryside liberally dotted with oak and pine. Six miles north of Mariposa is Mt. Bullion, named for John C. Fremont's father-in-law, Senator Thomas Hart Benton, whose nickname was "Old Bullion." Today Mt. Bullion is a tiny community with no facilities for travelers, but during the Gold Rush it was a busy place; $3 million in gold was taken from the nearby Princeton Mine. A few old buildings, including the *Trabucco Store* and the *Princeton Saloon*, are still standing. Beyond Mt. Bullion, SR 49 runs straight and fast to Bear Valley.

◆◆◆
SIDE TRIP TO HORNITOS

Rather than staying on SR 49, northbound motorists can take a scenic detour to Hornitos by leaving the main highway at Mt. Bullion, then rejoining it at Bear Valley; for southbound motorists, the order is reversed. From Mt. Bullion, it is about 13 miles to Hornitos, then 11 miles back to SR 49 at Bear Valley. Both side roads are fully paved, but each has sections that are steep, narrow and winding; one-way driving time via either route is about 25 minutes.

NOW Population 50; elevation 980 feet. There are no facilities for tourists.

Hornitos dozes peacefully in the bottom of a picturesque valley, its narrow streets leading past modest dwellings interspersed with dilapidated structures and deteriorating ruins that evoke its raucous past. Today Hornitos is rural, so much so that cattle occasionally wander onto the main street. The old plaza in front of the post office makes a good starting point for a walking tour of the village.

14

The *Ghirardelli Store*, now an interesting ruin, is located opposite the plaza. Built in 1859, it was operated by D. Ghirardelli Co., the well-known chocolate makers of San Francisco.

John Austerman

Facing Hornitos' small plaza is the former Merck's Saloon.

St. Catherine's Catholic Church, located atop a knoll overlooking Hornitos, dates from 1862. It was built of wood buttressed with stone and is now roofed with wooden shingles.

Other interesting remains of Hornitos' early days: The old *Hornitos Jail*, with its granite walls two feet thick . . . the *Hornitos School*, built in the 1860s, located just east of town on the road to Mt. Bullion . . . *Gagliardo's Store*, opened in 1854 . . . the *Masonic Lodge*, where by special dispensation meetings were held on the ground floor . . . remnants of a blacksmith shop.

THEN Hornitos is Spanish for "little ovens"; it refers to dome shaped rock and mud bake ovens that were used here. Hornitos came into being when American miners "voted" their Mexican counterparts out of nearby Quartzburg. Although Quartzburg was abandoned a short time later, Hornitos soon became one of the most wide-open, hell-raising towns in the Mother Lode. In its prime it had a population of 15,000 and supported four hotels, six stores, numerous saloons and fandango halls, and a Wells Fargo office that shipped $40,000 in gold a day. Tales of Hornitos' wicked ways were legend. One story concerned two fandango dancers who, armed with daggers, wrapped shawls around their arms and dueled to the death in the streets to the cheers of miners. Joaquin Murieta was said to have frequented Hornitos' saloons and fandango halls; a tunnel located near the north end of town supposedly served as his escape route.

◆◆◆
BEAR VALLEY

NOW Population 69; elevation 2050 feet. Facilities include a general store which provides gasoline and supplies.

15

Bear Valley is a hamlet with a scattering of old buildings and ruins lining the highway and a few aging homes along the back streets. Little physical evidence remains of the days when Col. John C. Fremont made Bear Valley the capital of his empire.

Among the interesting Gold Rush relics: The *I.O.O.F. Hall*, which today houses the Oso Museum (open on request; inquire at the store next door) . . . the *Trabucco Store*, first opened in 1862 . . . stone ruins on both sides of the highway . . . the large structure known a *Mrs. Trabucco's Mercantile*, built in 1880.

THEN In the early 1850s Bear Valley had a population of 3000 and was the home and headquarters of Col. John C. Fremont. Thanks to Fremont's wife Jessie, the town saw such Gold Rush rarities as a vegetable garden, French servants and elegant parties. Fremont built a home and a two-story, balconied hotel he named "Oso House"; nothing remains of either structure. In 1863 Fremont received $6 million for his Mariposa Grant; he had paid $3200 for it in 1847. When the mines declined, so did the town, leaving behind a shell of a once-prosperous gold camp.

John Austerman

After making a steep, corkscrew descent, SR 49 crosses the upper reaches of Lake McClure.

BEAR VALLEY TO COULTERVILLE
(16 miles, 35 minutes)

Just north of Bear Valley, SR 49 begins its long, twisting descent into the deep, spectacular canyon of the Merced River (locally known as "Hell's Hollow"). A turnout near the beginning of the steep downgrade provides a sweeping view of the chasm.

Near the bridge across the Merced River, a side road leads to the Bagby Recreation Area, featuring a campground and facilities for boating. This section of the river forms the upper reaches of Lake McClure. After climbing out of the gorge, SR 49 passes through rolling hills to Coulterville. There are no roadside facilities along this section, except for the campground.

COULTERVILLE

NOW Population 200; elevation 1740 feet. Lodging and camping facilities are available but limited. Other facilities include a rest area with a public pool, gas stations, a grocery store and several restaurants.

Coulterville is a picturesque community snugly situated in a small valley. Although SR 49 bisects what was once the plaza, most of the town lies east of the highway. Coulterville serves as the market center for the numerous small ranches that occupy the surrounding countryside. Despite three destructive fires and the depletion of gold in the area, Coulterville's residents have clung tenaciously to their community. Several of its original Gold Rush structures still stand; others are just walls of stone and brick, still guarded by iron doors and shutters.

The *Hotel Jeffery* is the most impressive building in Coulterville. It was originally built in the 1850s as a store with a Mexican dance hall on the second floor, then converted into a hotel in 1852; it was owned by the same family for three generations. Rebuilt more than once, it now has three stories, with walls 30 inches thick. It is now open year round, with 20 guest rooms furnished with antiques. Next door is the Magnolia Saloon, a restored Gold Rush-era barroom.

"Whistling Billy" the nickname for the locomotive that stands across SR 49 from the Jeffery Hotel under what was once Coulterville's hanging tree. This little engine was used to haul ore from the famous Mary Harrison Mine over four miles of what was called "the crookedest railroad in the world."

Sun Sun Wo Co., an adobe built in 1851, is the lone surviving remnant of Coulterville's once-extensive Chinatown. It is located near the east end of town on Chinatown Main St.

Northern Mariposa County History Center, located on the west side of SR 49, is housed in two brick and stone structures dating from 1856. Museum exhibits include historical photographs, early household utensils and a working scale model of a stamp mill. Open 10 a.m. to 4 p.m. daily, except Monday, April through October; weekends and some holidays the rest of the year; closed January.

Also of interest: The *Coulter Hotel*, once a four-story stone edifice . . . the *Barrett Blacksmith Shop*, built in the early 1850s, now a general store . . . the *Knights of Pythias Hall*, now a gift shop . . . the *I.O.O.F. Hall*, with its over-hanging balcony . . . the *Bruschi Bros. General Store*, built in 1853 of adobe, with walls two feet thick . . . the *Canova House*, built by Mexican stone masons in the 1860s . . . the *Public Cemetery*, set on a knoll on the east side of town, with some markers dating back nearly a century.

THEN In 1850 this was a predominantly Mexican mining town called *Banderita* ("little flag"), its name coming from the small American flag that adorned George Coulter's store. Ignoring the Mexican name, Coulter and fellow merchant George Maxwell drew lots to see whose name would be affixed to the town. Coulter won, but Maxwell's name was given to the creek that flows through the valley. Built near gold-rich quartz ledges and separated from other towns by miles of rugged terrain, Coulterville became an important supply center. Goods were delivered to the surrounding mines by pack train. At the height of the Gold Rush, Coulterville had a population of 5000, 1500 of whom were Chinese; 10 hotels and 25 saloons dispensed hospitality to travelers.

Tom Dell

Coulterville

18

Coulterville's last "gold rush" occurred in 1899, when a stone and adobe building was razed following a fire, and the rubble then used to fill potholes in the streets. Apparently a cache of gold coins had been hidden in the walls of the old building, because with the first rain, gold coins began to appear everywhere. The entire population turned out with everything from shovels to spoons, and the main street was soon reduced to a muddy trench.

COULTERVILLE TO CHINESE CAMP
(19 miles, 25 minutes)

Leaving Coulterville, SR 49 climbs gradually to a summit at the Mariposa-Tuolumne County line, then descends via sharp curves into the valley formed by the Tuolumne River. As it reaches the bottom of the grade, it passes the Moccasin Powerhouse, part of the Hetch Hetchy Aqueduct, the municipal water system for San Francisco. Just beyond the powerhouse is the junction with SR 120, which leads eastward to Big Oak Flat, Groveland and Yosemite National Park. Past this junction, SR 49 becomes a fast, modern highway with wide shoulders as it skirts Don Pedro Reservoir and winds through low, grass-covered hills to Chinese Camp.

◆◆◆

SIDE TRIP TO BIG OAK FLAT AND GROVELAND

Big Oak Flat and Groveland, a pair of old mining camps, lie six and eight miles, respectively, east of SR 49 on SR 120. One-way driving time from the junction is approximately 15 minutes to Big Oak Flat, 20 minutes to Groveland. Leaving SR 49 near the Moccasin Powerhouse complex, SR 120 makes a steep, corkscrew climb, gaining nearly 2000 feet in just over five miles, as brushy hillsides give way to pine-clad slopes. As the highway levels off, it passes the site of the historic *Priest Hotel*, now marked by a motel and cafe.

Big Oak Flat, at an elevation of 2803 feet, is a quiet village of 200 with a gas station, stores and limited accommodations. During the Gold Rush, however, it was a lively camp surrounded by rich placer deposits that yielded several million dollars in gold. A few old buildings still stand, including the two-story, iron-shuttered *I.O.O.F. Hall*, which dates from 1853 and is still in use. Just east of the hall stands a one-story stone-and-brick building from the 19th century that boasts a stone walkway and six large green doors made of iron. A monument near the west end of town displays pieces of wood from the original oak that gave the camp its name; the tree fell when miners dug away the gravel and earth around its base.

Groveland, once called *First Garrote*, was originally settled about 1850 by Mexican miners, who were subsequently driven away by Americans. It is today slightly larger than Big Oak Flat and also offers basic tourist facilities, including several bed and breakfast inns. Groveland's attractive main thoroughfare is lined with false-front and two-story turn-of-the-century structures. Among the buildings remaining from the Gold Rush is the *Iron Door Saloon*, built in 1852, still flourishing and claiming to be the oldest saloon in California.

CHINESE CAMP

NOW Population 150; elevation 1261 feet. Facilities consist of a small general store/gas station at the north edge of town.

Chinese Camp is a sleepy village located just west of SR 49. A number of old wood-frame houses line its streets, along with the decaying shells of several Gold Rush-era structures. On Red Hill Road, the modern Chinese Camp School, in keeping with the town's name, has a low, red, pagoda-style roof. The lacy tree of heaven, planted wherever Chinese miners settled, flourishes throughout the village. No Chinese live here today.

Interesting Gold Rush remains: The stone walls of the *Wells Fargo Building . . . St. Xavier Catholic Church*, perched on a hillside on the east side of the highway; it was erected in 1855 and restored in 1949 . . . *Timothy McAdams Store*, now an office of the Tuolumne County Visitors Bureau, (209) 984-4636.

THEN After being banished from nearby camps by intolerant Americans, a group of Chinese miners settled this area, which turned out to have rich gold deposits. By 1856 Chinese Camp had become the hub of a large network of transportation routes and boasted a population of 5000, most of whom were Chinese. During that year, the town was the scene of an event which became known as the Chinese Tong War. A disagreement among Chinese miners resulted in a full-scale battle between two tongs (secret Chinese societies). Preparations went on for several months, with all available blacksmiths for miles around commissioned to forge spears, knives and various crude weapons. Over 2100 Chinese were involved in the war, but since few firearms were used, only a handful of casualties occurred.

CHINESE CAMP TO JAMESTOWN
(6 miles, 8 minutes)

Just north of Chinese Camp, SR 120 branches off to the west and leads to the San Joaquin Valley. Past the junction, SR 49 continues to traverse grassy hillsides punctuated with stately oaks. Before reaching Jamestown, the highway crosses Woods Creek, which was the richest stream for its size in all of California. A town known as *Woods Crossing* sprang up here; in the mid-1850s it had a post office and two stamp mills, but no trace of it can be seen today. As SR 49 enters Jamestown, a side road branches off to the right and becomes the main street of the downtown area.

JAMESTOWN

NOW Population 2206; elevation 1405 feet. Facilities include bed and breakfast establishments and other lodgings, restaurants, gas stations, stores and other services.

Jamestown, with its brightly painted two-story buildings along the main street, is an oasis of antiquity. Despite losing a number of its original wood-frame buildings to a fire in 1966, "Jimtown" still sports several structures dating from the 1870s and 1880s. Most of these old balconied buildings are now occupied by various businesses, including a profusion of antique shops, many of which are closed on Tuesdays.

Railtown 1897 State Historic Park contains the original workshops and roundhouse of the Sierra Railway, which began operation more than 95 years ago. The park and its restored locomotives and railcars have been featured in more than 200 movies and television shows. The grounds are open daily from 10 a.m. to 5 p.m. Admission is free, and picnicking is permitted. Roundhouse tours are given every half hour 10:15 a.m. to 4:15 p.m.; fees are $2.50 for adults, $1.50 for ages 3-12. Excursions aboard steam-powered passenger trains are offered weekends March through November. Call for schedule and fares, (209) 984-3953.

The National Hotel on Main St., now a bed and breakfast, has been restored to its 19th-century appearance. Two stories and a balcony overlook Main Street, while inside, the original redwood long bar boasts a brass rail and an 1881 cash register.

The Jamestown Hotel on Main St. has been restored to its 1860s decor with period furnishings.

Other interesting buildings in Jamestown: *The Community Methodist Church*, on a hill one block east of the main street . . . the colorful *Emporium*, now an antique shop . . . an old *livery stable* on Main St., now housing an antique store and a gold shop where visitors can arrange a variety of prospecting expeditions. For information, call (209) 984-4653.

Tom Dell

Antique shops, like this one in Jamestown, abound in the Mother Lode country.

21

THEN   Col. George James, a San Francisco lawyer, founded Jamestown in 1848, shortly after gold was discovered along nearby Woods Creek. James left town under questionable circumstances the next year, and local miners tried to change the town's name to *American Camp*, to commemorate the banishment of Mexican miners from the diggings. When the post office was established in 1853, however, the original name was made official. "Jimtown" was sustained by rich quartz deposits that produced great quantities of gold long after the stream gravels were played out; at one time the population reached 6000. Local residents attempted to wrest the county seat away from neighboring Sonora, but they were unsuccessful. Mining continues today, with a large-scale mine in operation along the highway south of town.

JAMESTOWN TO SONORA
(4 miles, 5 minutes)

After leaving the northern edge of Jamestown, SR 49 almost immediately reaches the outskirts of Sonora. Rawhide Rd., which intersects SR 49 just north of Jamestown, provides a shortcut directly north to Angels Camp.

SONORA

NOW   Population 4200; elevation 1825 feet. There are numerous motels and bed and breakfast inns. Sonora offers a full range of facilities, including hospitals and a California State Automobile Association district office.

Sonora is a colorful, bustling little city with congested streets and two traffic signals. It is the seat of Tuolumne County and market center for a large area. Sonora's economy revolves around lumbering and agriculture, as well as tourism. The city's narrow streets wind up, down and across the slopes of several hills and along the bottom of steep-walled ravines. Although an air of progressive commercialism has been superimposed on this onetime rowdy mining camp, many relics from Sonora's flamboyant past remain, including a good collection of Victorian homes.

Sonora also marks the junction of SR 49 with SR 108, which provides access to recreation areas in the nearby Sierra Nevada. The city hosts the Mother Lode Round-Up every Mother's Day weekend and the Mother Lode Fair in July.

Tuolumne County Museum and History Center is housed in what once served as the town jail; it was originally constructed in 1857 and rebuilt in 1866 following a fire. The museum features an excellent collection of old photographs, along with other historical displays. The Tuolumne County Gold Collection, featuring nuggets and "free" gold, chronicles the history of gold mining in the county from Gold Rush days to the present. A restored cell block and its small, domed jail cells now contain a gun collection, a replica of a gun shop and an exhibit recounting early settlers' arduous journeys west. The building is also occupied by the Tuolumne County Genealogy Society. The museum is open 10 a.m. to 4 p.m. Monday through Saturday; additional summer hours, Sunday 10 a.m. to 3:30 p.m. Located on West Bradford St., two blocks northwest of SR 49. (209) 532-1317.

St. James Episcopal Church, located near the north end of town on SR 49, was built in 1860 and is said to be the second oldest Episcopal church of frame construction in California. Considered by many to be the most beautiful frame building in the

Mother Lode, it continues to serve an active congregation. Unlike the typical white Mother Lode church, St. James is painted a striking dark red.

The Gunn House, built in 1850, served as the home of Dr. Lewis C. Gunn, then as the office of the Sonora Herald—the area's first newspaper. It has been remodeled and now is operated as a motel; its rooms feature antique furnishings. Located on Washington St. (SR 108), two blocks south of SR 49.

St. Patrick's Catholic Church, originally built in 1862, destroyed by fire in 1874 and then rebuilt, is located one block west of the courthouse on Jackson St. Its tall white steeple is visible from nearly anywhere in Sonora.

The *I.O.O.F. Hall* is a two-story brick building dating from 1853. It has been remodeled and is still in use. Located near the north end of Washington St. (SR 49).

Several *Victorian houses* can be seen on Sonora's *Heritage Home Tour*, a walking tour that takes in a dozen of these interesting old residences. The tour begins at the Tuolumne County Museum, where a descriptive brochure of Sonora's historical sites sells for a nominal fee.

The *Street-Morgan Mansion*, one of the most beautiful old homes in the Mother Lode, was designed in an intricate, elegant Victorian style. It is painted the same dark red as St. James Episcopal Church, which is directly across the street. Its rooms now serve as business offices.

John Austerman

The historic Tuolumne County Courthouse is one of several architectural treasures found in Sonora.

Also of interest: The *Tuolumne County Courthouse*, built in 1898 . . . the *Opera Hall*, dating from 1870 . . . the *Sugg-McDonald House*, the original portion built in 1857 . . . four cemeteries, all founded in the 1850s . . . several business structures on Washington St., each over a hundred years old.

THEN Sonora, known as "Queen of the Southern Mines," was the biggest, richest and wildest town in the southern Mother Lode. It was settled in 1848 by miners from Sonora, Mexico, who found fabulous gold deposits here. The camp almost immediately mushroomed into a Latin-flavored metropolis with adobe houses, fandango halls and bullbaiting. Soon, however, American miners learned of the golden treasure of *Sonorian Camp*; they were incensed to find "foreigners" working the rich diggings. The resulting racial strife saw many of the Mexicans becoming outlaws, raiding, robbing and murdering the Yankees who attempted to steal their claims. Lawlessness was rampant, and no one walked Sonora's streets unarmed. The situation came to a climax when the state legislature passed a law requiring foreign miners to pay a monthly tax of $20 per man. The law was enforced with guns, and Sonora soon got what it wanted—the departure of some 2000 Mexicans. Ironically, the tax proved to be the end of Sonora as a boomtown; things became so quiet, in fact, that the local newspaper folded for lack of patrons.

The tax on foreign miners was repealed in 1851, but Sonora never regained its pre-tax wickedness. Instead it became known for its orderliness and civilized character. Enough gold remained in the mines of Tuolumne County to sustain the town. Four devastating fires brought widespread destruction, but Sonora always bounced back. Its proximity to the major supply center of Stockton made it an important transportation center, while nearby forests and ranches brought additional economic wealth. By the time the mines finally gave out, Sonora's permanence was assured.

This giant wooden wheel was used to move tailings from Jackson's Kennedy Mine, which is seen in the background.

Central Mother Lode

NOW This is the heart of the Mother Lode country, containing more old mining communities than the southern and northern sections combined. Every few miles along SR 49 is another interesting Gold Rush camp; some are now modern and progressive towns, while others are deteriorating monuments to their past glories. The land is gently rolling, with a sparse cover of oak and pine. Elevations range from about 600 feet to just over 2000 feet. Summers are hot and dry, while winters are usually mild, although snow occasionally falls in the upper elevations. Spring wildflowers and fall foliage add touches of color to the landscape.

THE ROAD Along this 102-mile section, SR 49 alternately crosses rolling plateaus and the deep river gorges that separate them. Driving conditions are generally good, although some stretches are narrow and winding. Important east-west routes lead westward to Stockton and Sacramento and east into the Sierra Nevada. Good side roads lead to Columbia, Murphys, Volcano, Fiddletown and Georgetown; each side trip is worth the few extra miles, particularly Columbia. For detailed road information, refer to the CSAA *Lake Tahoe Region* map.

FACILITIES Sonora, Jackson, Placerville and Auburn offer abundant accommodations and services for travelers; each makes an excellent base for sightseeing. Campgrounds and trailer spaces are limited along SR 49, although they are plentiful both east and west of the highway. See the AAA *California/Nevada TourBook* or the California State Automobile Association's *Bed and Breakfast* book for accommodations listings. For camping information refer to the AAA *CampBook* or the ACSC *Central and Southern* and *Northern California Camping* maps.

RECREATION The Sierra Nevada offers a wide range of recreational activities, including winter sports. White-water rafting is popular on some rivers, and nearby reservoirs lure boating enthusiasts.

THEN The first discovery of gold in the Mother Lode region occurred here. Most miners concentrated on placer gold, although rich quartz deposits provided additional wealth. Since the close of the gold era, cattle, lumber and tourism have kept many Central Mother Lode communities from fading into oblivion.

SIDE TRIP TO COLUMBIA STATE HISTORIC PARK

Two miles past Sonora, SR 49 reaches the junction with Parrotts Ferry Rd., which leads northward another two miles to Columbia State Historic Park. Parrotts Ferry Rd. continues northward and provides an alternate to SR 49. Beyond Columbia, it crosses New Melones Lake, passes the road to Moaning Cavern and meets SR 4 at Vallecito; here motorists can return to SR 49 at Angels Camp or proceed eastward via SR 4 to Murphys. From Columbia, it is 14 miles to either Angels Camp or Murphys; driving time is approximately 25 minutes.

NOW Population 1000; elevation 2143 feet. Facilities include several motels, bed and breakfast inns and camping areas; restaurants are good but limited. Picnic facilities are found throughout the park.

Columbia is the best-preserved gold mining town in California and, for many visitors, the top attraction in the Mother Lode country. This is the result of two important factors: first, when two disastrous fires in the 1850s destroyed much of Columbia, the town was rebuilt primarily of brick, and many of its Gold Rush-era structures survived. Second, in 1945 the State began a program of acquisition and renovation in Columbia, preserving most of the town as a state historic park.

Today Columbia is a living museum of the past. Along its tree-lined streets are dozens of authentically reproduced businesses of the 1850s and 1860s. On a stroll down the shady boardwalks, you can peer into an old-time pharmacy, newspaper office or saddlemaker's shop; watch a wooden coach take shape in the blacksmith's shop; or sip a sarsaparilla in a restored saloon. Wares are sold by shopkeepers dressed in the costumes of Columbia's Gold Rush heyday. Columbia attracts thousands of visitors, and the town often becomes crowded in summer, taking on an amusement park atmosphere that some history buffs find annoying. But beneath its commercial veneer, Columbia offers so much historical authenticity that it is the closest thing possible to a step backward in time. The main street is closed to traffic, making the town an excellent place for walking. A brochure outlining a self-guided tour of Columbia can be obtained at the park museum or the ranger office.

John Austerman

Columbia State Historic Park is a living museum of the Gold Rush.

27

Columbia holds an Easter parade, and in May the colorful Fireman's Muster features competition between old hand-pumped fire engines. During the summer a college repertory company performs plays at the Fallon House Theater. From June through September, visitors can tour an operating gold mine; a courtesy bus departs from Main St. Other annual events include The Columbia Diggin's in June, a festive July Fourth celebration and performances of *A Miner's Christmas* in December.

The Museum is housed in the Knapp Building, a single-story brick structure erected in 1854 as a miner's supply store. Various relics from Columbia's early days are on display, and a narrated slide show is given periodically. Open 8 a.m. to 5 p.m. daily. Located at Main and State sts.

John Austerman

Stagecoach rides depart from the Wells Fargo Express Building in Columbia.

The Wells Fargo Express Building is a two-story brick structure with iron shutters and fancy grillwork edging its small balcony. It was built in 1858. The ground-floor interior has been restored to approximate its original appearance; it contains a display relating to commerce in early-day Columbia. Stagecoach and surrey rides depart from in front of the Wells Fargo Building daily during the summer and weekends the rest of the year.

The City Hotel was first opened in 1856. It was fully restored in 1975 and now serves as a training facility for hotel-management students from nearby Columbia Community College. Nine guest rooms are furnished with antiques; the hotel also features a saloon and an elegant dining room that is open nightly except Monday.

Fallon Hotel, adjoining the Fallon House Theater, offers lodging in a Victorian setting. Like the City Hotel, it also serves as a training facility.

Fallon House Theater is the scene of plays presented by Columbia Actors Repertory group. The red brick building dates from 1860.

The *I.O.O.F. Hall*, at State St. and Broadway, was built as a grocery store in 1855. Since 1857, however, it has served as the Odd Fellows' meeting hall.

Columbia Gazette Office is a replica of the original newspaper office, which was built in 1855. The Gazette is still an operating newspaper. Downstairs are displays relating to early printing.

St. Anne's Catholic Church sits atop a knoll at the south edge of town. A brick structure with a tall, square belfry, St. Anne's was begun in 1852 and finished in 1857; it is one of California's oldest brick churches.

The Schoolhouse, a functional, block-shaped structure at the north end of town, was one of California's first public schools. It was built in 1860 and restored 100 years later. Behind the schoolhouse is the old Columbia Cemetery, begun in 1853.

Other attractions: The small, sturdy *Jail*, which visitors can enter . . . the *Columbia House*, a period restaurant . . . replicas of the *First Presbyterian Church* and the *Masonic Temple* . . . the working *Blacksmith Shop* . . . the *Eagle Cotage*, a white frame structure with a historically misspelled name, now used as a dormitory for theatrical groups performing at the Fallon House Theater . . . two *firehouses*, each displaying an old-time "hand-pumper" fire engine purchased in San Francisco.

THEN Columbia got off to a somewhat later start than most Mother Lode boomtowns, but its great wealth and phenomenal growth soon overcame this handicap. When Dr. Thaddeus Hildreth and his party found gold here in March of 1850, they managed to gather 30 pounds of nuggets in two days. Within a month, some 5000 miners had turned *Hildreth's Diggin's* into a bustling collection of tents and shanties. The camp's name was soon changed to *American Camp* and then to Columbia. Despite its wealth, early-day Columbia suffered from a lack of water, which was indispensable for placer mining. As a result, two water companies built an intricate system of ditches and flumes, including a 60-mile-long aqueduct.

Fire was another problem. In 1854 the entire business district—except the single brick building—burned down. During the ensuing reconstruction, brick was used extensively, along with iron doors and shutters. By this time Columbia had become a town of 5000 inhabitants and was California's second-largest city. It boasted four banks, eight hotels, two fire companies, three churches, a school, three theaters, 53 stores, 40 saloons and 159 gambling dens. The supply of gold seemed inexhaustible; the earth was so laced with gold that claims in some sections were limited to plots 10 feet square. But by 1870, after some 2.5 million ounces of gold had been taken out, the gold was gone, and Columbia became a nearly abandoned shell.

29

SONORA TO ANGELS CAMP
(16 miles, 25 minutes)

Beyond the turnoff to Columbia, SR 49 winds through rolling farm country to Tuttletown, where a historic plaque stands next to the stone ruins of Swerer's Store, built in 1852 and patronized by Mark Twain. A mile past Tuttletown, a paved side road leads 3/4 mile to Mark Twain's cabin on Jackass Hill and affords some sweeping views of New Melones Lake along the way. The cabin is a replica built around the original chimney. (A few picnic tables have been added to the property.) During his stay here in 1864-65, Twain penned "The Celebrated Jumping Frog of Calaveras County" and *Roughing It*. Next is the turnoff to Tuttletown Recreation Area, offering camping and facilities for boating on New Melones Lake. A high, modern bridge whisks travelers across the reservoir, which in recent years has experienced a dramatic drop in its water level resulting from a prolonged drought. During the Gold Rush the crossing was made via the old *Robinson's Ferry*, which served the booming camp of Melones. The site of the ferry and the town were inundated by the reservoir.

John Austerman

SR 49 crosses the upper reaches of New Melones Lake via this modern bridge.

After crossing the bridge, SR 49 climbs into rolling pastureland and soon reaches Carson Hill, now a tiny hamlet, but during the Gold Rush perhaps the single richest spot in the Mother Lode. The nearby Morgan Mine produced $5 million from a hole twelve feet long, six feet wide and eight feet deep; a 195-pound nugget, largest ever mined in California, was found here in 1854. Just north of Carson Hill, the well-preserved stone shell of an imposing structure stands alongside the highway. This is the *Romaggi Home* (1852), last remnant of a camp called *Albany Flat*. SR 49 winds past the entrance to the Calaveras County Fairgrounds and, across the highway, the entrance to Glory Hole Recreation Area with camp-grounds and boating facilities. The highway then continues into Angels Camp. Along the stretch of highway between the turnoff to Columbia and Angels Camp are a store at Tuttletown, a viewpoint at the north end of the New Melones Reservoir bridge and a rest area at Carson Hill.

ANGELS CAMP

NOW Population 2811; elevation 1379 feet. Lodging, including bed and break-fast inns, and restaurants are available. Other facilities for travelers are plentiful and include a California State Automobile Association district office.

Angels Camp, incorporated in 1912, is a compact community built along the bottom and sides of a ravine. Narrow lanes angle off here and there over the hilly terrain, and high curbstones help compensate for varying ground levels. Many of the business establishments lining SR 49 (which serves as the main street) sport the iron shutters, fancy brickwork and overhanging balconies of the Gold Rush era, but the atmosphere is generally one of practicality. Every year during the third week of May, however, Angels Camp assumes an air of frivoli-ty as it celebrates the Annual Jumping Frog Jubilee; this famous event, held at the fairgrounds south of town, coincides with the Calaveras County Fair. Angels Camp also hosts a gem and mineral show in March, the Calaveras County Fair and International Jumping Frog Jubilee in May, in July the Mark Twain July 4th Celebration and Fireworks Show and in September a festival in honor of the zucchini. A walking-tour map of the town is available at the Calaveras County Visitor Information Center.

Mark Twain, memorialized by this statue in Angels Camp, made the town famous with his story "The Celebrated Jumping Frog of Calaveras County."

Angels Camp Museum is located on SR 49 a mile north of the town center. Outdoors is a collection of old mining equipment and minerals of the Mother Lode. Among the displays inside are 19th-century household items and mining

31

tools, a horse-drawn hearse, magic lantern and a working model of a stamp mill. A carriage house and sheds behind the main museum contain a large collection of horse-drawn vehicles, farm and logging equipment, a combination blacksmith and carriage shop, and a mineral collection. There is a shaded picnic area on the grounds. The entire complex is open 10 a.m. to 3 p.m. daily April through Thanksgiving weekend; open Wednesday through Sunday the rest of the year. Admission is $1 for adults, 25¢ for children 6-12. For additional information, call (209) 736-2963.

Angels Hotel, located on Main St. near the south end of town, is a two-story, iron-shuttered structure built in 1855. Here Mark Twain is reported to have heard the story that formed the basis for his tale of "The Celebrated Jumping Frog of Calaveras County."

Also of interest: The *I.O.O.F. Building*, a two-story stone structure . . . the statue of Mark Twain in Utica Park.

THEN George Angel was a member of the party that discovered gold here in 1848, but Angel was a merchant, not a miner. He founded a trading post and gave the camp its name. Gold was plentiful around Angels Camp; by 1849 some 4500 miners were prospecting the area, and many rich strikes were reported. Angel prospered too, since a shirt sold for $50 and tools for up to $200 each. When the placer gold eventually gave out, a man by the unlikely name of Bennager Rasberry saved the day. While out hunting one day, his ramrod stuck in his gun, so he shot it into the ground, revealing a large piece of gold-bearing quartz. In three days Rasberry mined $10,000, and the boom was on again. The quartz deposits in the area made Angels Camp one of the richest towns in the Mother Lode.

Angels Camp inevitably faded when the supply of gold dwindled. But this was Mark Twain-Bret Harte country, and the two writers made the name of Angels Camp a byword that still evokes the spirit of the Gold Rush.

SIDE TRIP TO MURPHYS

Travelers who wish to visit the charming old town of Murphys have a choice of two routes, which together make possible an interesting loop trip. SR 4, which leaves SR 49 in Angels Camp, is the quickest. One-way distance to Murphys is nine miles; driving time is about 12 minutes. Five miles east of Angels Camp is the pleasant little tree-shaded village of Vallecito, once a Mexican mining camp. Two Gold Rush-era structures—the *Wells Fargo Office* (now in ruins) and the *Dinkenspiel Store*—sit in the center of the village.

Moaning Cavern, two miles south of Vallecito, is a colorful limestone cavern explored by gold miners in 1851. Cave visitors can choose to descend by steps or by a 180-foot rope. Open for guided tours 9 a.m. to 6 p.m. daily in summer and 10 a.m. to 5 p.m. during winter; admission is $5.75 for adults; $2.75 for ages 6-12 and free for ages 5 and under. A **discount** is offered to AAA or CAA members; see *California/Nevada TourBook* for details. A three-hour spelunking trip can also be arranged; reservations are required. For information and reservations, call (209) 736-2708.

The second route connecting SR 49 with Murphys is the Murphys Grade Rd., somewhat slower than SR 4 but more scenic. Heading west from Murphys, it follows a rushing creek and an old flume for a few miles, then crosses attractive farming country to its junction with SR 49 at Altaville; the seven miles can be driven in about 15 minutes.

NOW Population 2200; elevation 2171 feet. Lodging and dining facilities are available, including a bed and breakfast inn. Gasoline and supplies are also available.

John Austerman

Murphys Hotel, which dates from 1856, offers Victorian-style accommodations in the original building, as well as more contemporary furnishings in an adjacent lodge.

Murphys, one of the most captivating communities in the Mother Lode, is a well-preserved relic of the 19th century. Its main street is lined with interesting old buildings dating from the Gold Rush. Aside from automobiles, paved streets and a profusion of wine-tasting establishments, Murphys makes few concessions to the 20th century. The village is compact, and its pleasant, tree-shaded streets invite leisurely exploration on foot. Murphys is usually quiet and uncrowded, except during the third week of July, when it hosts its Annual Homecoming Celebration. In March is Irish Day, and during the months of April and November the local Black Bart Players perform musicals, comedies and old-time melodramas in the Black Bart Playhouse. On the first Sunday of October is Gold Rush Day.

Murphys Hotel is the most imposing restored old building in town. Opened in 1856 as the Sperry and Perry Hotel, the name of the hotel has changed, but its 19th-century atmosphere remains. Its front door still bears bullet scars dating from Murphys' lively heyday; a photocopy of the old register bears such famous names as Mark Twain, Horatio Alger, Ulysses S. Grant, C.E. Bolton (better known as Black Bart) and Thomas Lipton (the tea magnate).

Peter L. Traver Building, across the street from the Murphys Hotel at the end of the block, was constructed in 1856. Inside the stone structure is the *Old Timers Museum*, which houses a collection of Gold Rush memorabilia. Open to the public Friday through Sunday 11 a.m. to 4 p.m. Admission is 50¢ for adults, 25¢ for children over 6. Behind the building is a blacksmith shop, old wagons and other items of interest.

Wall of Comparative Ovations, on the west outside wall of the Old Timers Museum, was erected by E Clampus Vitus, a combination humor and benevolent society founded during the Gold Rush and revived by historians in the 1930s. The wall displays plaques commemorating the deeds of pioneers and members of the society.

Murphys Grammar School sits on a hill near the corner of Main and Jones streets. Known as "Pine Tree College," it first opened in 1860. Until its close in 1973, it was California's oldest public school. One of its graduates, Albert Michelson, won the Nobel Prize for physics in 1907.

Mercer Caverns, open to visitors since 1885, are located a mile north of Murphys. Forty-five-minute tours take visitors past fanciful limestone formations. Open 9 a.m. to 5 p.m. daily June through September, 11 a.m. to 4 p.m. weekends and school holidays during the rest of the year; visitors should arrive in time to complete the tour before closing time. Admission is $5 for adults, $2.50 for children 5-11; rates subject to change. (Arrive early in summer; weekends often sell out.) A **discount** is offered to AAA or CAA members; see *California/Nevada TourBook* for details.

John Austerman

Thorpe's Bakery Building in Murphys dates from 1859. Murphys, like many gold country communities, suffered disastrous fires. Many of the structures that remain were built of stone.

Other historic buildings in Murphys: *The Fisk Building* (1859) began as a saloon, later served as post office and now houses three businesses . . . *Masonic Temple*, a two-story, white-frame structure located on Church St., one block north of Main . . . *First Congregational Church*, at Church and Algiers sts., dates from 1895 . . . *Sperry House*, dating from the 1850s . . . *Thorpe's Bakery*, rebuilt of stone after the fire of 1859 . . . *St. Patrick's Catholic Church* (1858), located on the edge of town . . . the

Jones Apothecary Shop, built in 1860 . . . *Compere Building*, built in the late 1850s, now a private residence . . . the *Stangetti Store* (1881), a stone structure with a wooden annex built in 1907.

THEN John and Daniel Murphy came west in 1844 with the first emigrant party to cross the Sierra Nevada with wagons. They began as Indian traders, but after hearing of the discovery of gold on the American River, turned to prospecting. In July 1848, they moved to a site near Angels Creek, where they made a rich strike. After putting 150 Indians to work on their claims, the Murphy brothers opened a trading post that took in as much as $400 a day in gold dust. The camp, first known as *Murphys New Diggin's*, grew rapidly. By the end of 1849, the Murphys had made a fortune and left town. The camp continued to prosper: in less than 10 years, the local Wells Fargo office shipped over $15 million in gold. At its peak Murphys could claim 3000 inhabitants, more than 500 frame houses, two restaurants, an express and banking house, a livery stable, blacksmith and carpenter shops, bakeries, butcher shops, two steam-powered sawmills, a cider and syrup factory, a bowling alley, eight busy taverns, and numerous dance halls and bawdy houses. As a result of fires which ravaged Murphys in 1859, 1874 and 1893, many stone buildings were constructed here.

ANGELS CAMP TO SAN ANDREAS
(12 miles, 15 minutes)

A mile north of historic Angels Camp is a community once known as Altaville, site of California's first iron foundry. Today the town is incorporated with Angels Camp as the city of Angels. Of historical note are the *Prince and Garibardi Store* (1857), a block-shaped stone structure with iron doors and shutters, now housing two shops, and the red brick *Altaville School*, built in 1858 and used until 1950. Altaville is also the site of the "discovery" of the celebrated Pliocene skull in a mine in 1866; it later turned out to be an intricate hoax perpetrated by local residents. Midway between Altaville and San Andreas is the site of *Fourth Crossing*, a former boom camp. Little remains here today, but during the Gold Rush this was the scene of rich placer deposits and a busy stage and freight depot. For the remainder of the way to San Andreas, SR 49 passes through scenic, mostly level farm country.

SAN ANDREAS

NOW Population 2150; elevation 1008 feet. Limited lodging and dining facilities include a bed and breakfast inn; ample services can be found, including a hospital and an airfield.

San Andreas, seat of Calaveras County, has something of a split personality. The section fronting SR 49 is relatively modern in appearance, but the downtown area (east of the main highway—signed "Historic") presents a 19th-century facade. Several old buildings line the main street, and narrow lanes twist up and down low hills.

35

Calaveras County Museum and Archives comprises three historic buildings: the *I.O.O.F. Hall* (1856), the *Hall of Records* and the old *Courthouse*. One area on the second floor of the courthouse is devoted to a comprehensive display of Miwok Indian history and artifacts. A large adjoining room contains photographs and household and farming objects that reveal life in pioneer mining days. The museum is open 10 a.m. to 4 p.m. daily. Admission is 50¢ for adults, 25¢ for children. Also of interest are the courtroom where Black Bart was tried in 1883 and the old jail where he awaited trial.

California Caverns are located 11 miles east of San Andreas at Cave City. Eighty-minute guided tours take visitors through narrow passageways and large chambers containing interesting calcite formations. Flat-heeled shoes are recommended. Tours are offered daily, departing every hour between 10 a.m. and 5 p.m. in summer; weekends and holidays in winter (weather permitting). Admission is $5.75 for adults, $2.75 for children 6-12; children under 5 years are free. A **discount** is offered to AAA or CAA members; see *California/Nevada Tourbook* for details. Spelunking trips lasting two to four hours can also be arranged; reservations are required. For information and reservations call (209) 736-2708.

The small hillside *Pioneer Cemetery*, dating from 1851, is located alongside SR 12, about one mile northwest of San Andreas.

THEN San Andreas began in 1848 as a Mexican mining camp. When American miners learned of the rich gold deposits, they swarmed into the camp and drove away the "foreigners." One of the Mexicans ejected from San Andreas, according to many accounts, was Joaquin Murieta, who retaliated against racial abuse by turning to a career as a terrorist outlaw. San Andreas also witnessed strife between American and French miners, resulting in the departure of the Frenchmen. After winning a heated battle with Mokelumne Hill, San Andreas became the county seat in 1866.

Black Bart's days as a highwayman came to an end here. He was caught in 1883 after 28 bloodless stagecoach robberies over a period of eight years. After pleading guilty, Bart was sent to San Quentin, where he served his sentence and then was never heard from again.

SAN ANDREAS TO MOKELUMNE HILL
(8 miles, 10 minutes)

This stretch of SR 49 winds through gently rolling countryside containing small farms and cattle ranches. Seven miles beyond San Andreas is *Chili Gulch*, now a peaceful little valley but in 1849 the scene of the "Chilean War," another struggle between American miners and their foreign-born counterparts. The dispute arose when the Americans passed a law banning the Chilean leaders' practice of using peon laborers to work their claims. The ensuing armed conflict was won by the Americans. SR 49 bypasses the center of Mokelumne Hill, but a side road (signed "Historic 49") loops through the village, rejoining the main highway after one mile.

MOKELUMNE HILL

NOW   Population 560; elevation 1474 feet. Limited lodging facilities, and a few restaurants can be found. Other facilities include gas stations and stores.

"Mok Hill" is today a tiny, tranquil shell of what once was one of the largest and most violent towns in the Mother Lode. Many of its remaining Gold Rush relics are slowly giving in to picturesque decay, but a few old buildings are still in use. The sleepy village awakens every July 4, when it holds its Annual Independence Day Parade.

The *I.O.O.F. Hall* is a three-story stone structure looming dramatically at the north end of the main street. It was built with two stories in 1854; the third floor was added in 1861.

The *Hotel Leger*, originally the Hotel de France (1851), was rebuilt by George Leger after a fire in 1854, only to burn down and be rebuilt again in 1874. It has been restored and now operates as a bed and breakfast inn. A handsome wooden balcony runs the length of the second story. The *Courthouse*, added as a wing of the hotel after the 1874 fire, served as the seat of Calaveras County from 1855 to 1866.

Other interesting historic sites: *Mokelumne Hill Community Church*, built in 1856 . . . the ruins of the *L. Mayer & Son Store*, which dates from 1854 . . . the single-story *Wells Fargo Office*, constructed of stone in 1865 . . . the *Protestant Cemetery* (1851), located at the north end of town.

THEN   After a group of miners found gold along the banks of the Mokelumne River in 1848, one of them opened a trading post on a hill above the river. Within four years, Mokelumne Hill had become a busy, booming camp and seat of Calaveras County. Gold proved to be so abundant here that claims were restricted to plots 16 feet square. Diverse ethnic groups made up the population of the camp, and racial abuse was common. So was violence. After the "Chilean War" of 1849 was settled, the "French War" took place on nearby French Hill, where miners from France had made a rich strike. In their exuberance, they raised the tricolor atop the hill. This gave avaricious American miners the excuse they needed to drive the Frenchmen from the hill and appropriate their claims. Robberies and killings were rampant; during one 17-week period, at least one murder per week was recorded.

During the 1860s the gold began to give out, and the population dwindled. After losing the county seat to San Andreas in 1866, Mokelumne Hill began to fade, eventually becoming the placid village it is today.

MOKELUMNE HILL TO JACKSON
(8 miles, 10 minutes)

After leaving the junction with the main street of Mokelumne Hill, SR 49 descends to a bridge crossing the Mokelumne River, where it enters Amador County. As it climbs out of the heavily wooded river canyon, the highway passes the two-story stone shell of the *Butte Store*, the lone remnant of the mining camp of Butte City. SR 49 enters Jackson—the center of town is just east of the highway.

37

JACKSON

NOW Population 3900; elevation 1200 feet. Lodging and dining facilities are plentiful, including several bed and breakfast establishments. A wide range of services can be found in and around Jackson, including a hospital, an airfield and a California State Automobile Association district office.

A sprawling community with an air of progress superimposed on its mining-camp heritage, Jackson is surrounded by rolling hills dotted with old mines. The colorful heart of Jackson comprises busy streets and well-kept old buildings. Surrounding the city center are residential districts where narrow, tree-shaded streets wind past fine old homes. Jackson has served as Amador County seat since the formation of the county in 1854. Lumbering, stock raising, tourism and agriculture, including a growing wine industry, sustain the local economy. Jackson's annual Dandelion Days Celebration and Flea Market is held in March.

The *Amador County Museum* is housed in the historic *Brown House*, a refurbished brick edifice constructed in 1859 and located on Church St. at the eastern edge of downtown. The two-story museum contains a variety of exhibits, including late 19th-century clothing, utensils, furniture and musical instruments. Open 10 a.m. to 4 p.m. Wednesday through Sunday. Donation. A separate building contains detailed working models of the Kennedy Mine operations; hours of operation vary. Admission is $1 for adults, 50¢ for children ages 6-12. Also, a third building at 38 Summit St. houses historical records and archives. Open 10 a.m. to 4 p.m. Friday. Admission free. (209) 223-6386; archives (209) 223-6389.

The National Hotel was built on the site of the *Louisiana House* after a fire destroyed the town in 1862. The hotel is still in business and is one of California's oldest continuously operated hostelries. On the ground floor is a tavern and in the basement a restaurant.

St. Sava Church, on N. Main St. north of the downtown area, is a stately church presiding over a well-kept cemetery. Built in 1894, it is the mother church in North America of the Serbian Orthodox faith.

First Congregational, Murphys

St. Sava, Jackson

Churches of the Mother Lode

St. James, Sonora

St. Joseph's, Mariposa

St. Xavier, Chinese Camp

The Kennedy Tailings Wheels, four giant wooden wheels 58 feet in diameter, were built in 1913 to transport tailings from the nearby Kennedy Mine to an impoundment; the 2000-foot-long system could move 850 tons per day. Two of the huge wheels still stand in a park located on Jackson Gate Rd. north of downtown. From the parking area, trails lead to the wheels.

The Kennedy and Argonaut Mines were two of the deepest and most productive gold mines in the United States. Together they produced more than $70 million in gold from the rich quartz veins which reached more than a mile into the earth. The headframes and mine buildings can be seen from various viewpoints, but the mine sites are closed to the public.

Also of interest: The *I.O.O.F. Hall* (1863), reputedly the tallest three-story structure in the United States . . . a sidewalk plaque on Main St. marking the former location of the *Hanging Tree* . . . *St. Patrick's Catholic Church* and *United Methodist Church*, both built in the 1860s . . . the *Chichizola Store*, dating from the 1850s, located near the Kennedy Tailings Wheels . . . cemeteries on the north side of town, with some markers dating back to the mid-19th century . . . *Vista Point* north of town off both sides of SR 49, affording a good view of the town and the headframes of once-flourishing gold mines.

THEN Jackson never had rich placer deposits, and water—not gold—was initially the reason for its existence. Topography provided a natural ford where the forks of a small creek came together. A dependable spring made this a natural way station for thirsty travelers. A sizable accumulation of bottles resulted, causing Mexican miners to name the place *Botilleas*. The camp soon became a trade and transportation center. By late 1849 its name had been changed to Jackson Creek, after either President Andrew Jackson or a merchant named Alden Jackson.

Jackson grew rapidly to become the rival of nearby Mokelumne Hill. Jackson was the seat of Calaveras County from 1851 to 1852, and its citizens later led a movement to form Amador County in 1854.

Placer gold, never abundant, soon gave out, but rich quartz deposits were discovered in the early 1850s. The Kennedy and Argonaut mines, along with a few smaller producers, were mainstays of the local economy until they closed in 1942. Although the closure of the mines dealt Jackson a severe blow, income from agriculture, lumbering and tourism has kept the town alive.

◆◆◆

SIDE TRIP TO VOLCANO

Four separate routes, all of them scenic, connect SR 49 with the charming Gold Rush village of Volcano; together, they offer several loop trip possibilities. SR 88 from Jackson and Ridge Rd., which leads eastward from SR 49 just north of Martell, converge at Pine Grove, where gasoline, supplies and limited accommodations can be found. The Pine Grove-Volcano Rd. branches north here and passes Indian Grinding Rock State Historic Park en route to Volcano. Total distance to Volcano via SR 88 is about 12 miles; one-way driving time is approximately 17 minutes. The Ridge Rd. route, which winds along the top of a ridge offering many scenic views, is a mile longer and takes about 22 minutes to drive.

Tom Dell

Indian Grinding Rock State Historic Park is California's only state park devoted to American Indian culture. Here Miwok tribesmen left petroglyphs and hundreds of mortar holes on a rock outcropping.

The other two routes to Volcano leave SR 49 at Sutter Creek. The more direct route is via Sutter Creek-Volcano Rd., which follows a creek through a wooded valley for 12 miles; it can be driven in about 20 minutes. Gopher Flat Rd. becomes Shake Ridge Rd. and leads 13 miles from Sutter Creek to *Daffodil Hill*, where colorful displays of flowers occur every spring. From Daffodil Hill, the Ram's Horn Grade descends three miles to Volcano; driving time from Sutter Creek to Volcano via Daffodil Hill is about 30 minutes.

Indian Grinding Rock State Historic Park, located on the road connecting Pine Grove with Volcano, is California's only state park devoted primarily to Indian culture. Here the Chaw'se Regional Indian Museum houses artifacts that represent the Miwok and neighboring tribes. Group tours and informative films are offered, and demonstrations are given by the Chaw'se Association and Amador Tribal Council. Each year on the weekend following the fourth Friday of September, various Native American tribes gather here for "Big Time," when the old ways are celebrated with dances, games, arts and crafts, and sharing of many traditional foods.

Before the Gold Rush, this was a seasonal meeting place of the Miwok Indians, hunters and gatherers who lived along the western slope of the Sierra Nevada. A limestone outcropping, set in a grassy meadow dotted with huge, spreading oaks, was used by the Miwoks as a mortar for grinding acorn meal; nearly 1200 mortar holes have been ground into the 7700-square-foot rock, and petroglyphs have been etched onto its surface. Nearby are replicas of Indian dwellings and the regional Indian museum. The park also features campsites. Day use is $5 per car; campsites are $12-$14.

41

NOW Population 99; elevation 2053 feet. Lodging can be found at a historic hotel and its adjacent motel. Volcano has a small store, a cafe and a few shops.

Volcano is a picturesque village set in a bowl-shaped depression surrounded by pine-covered hills. Except in spring when Daffodil Hill is in bloom and in midsummer, when hundreds of tourists come to enjoy the 19th-century ambience, Volcano slumbers peacefully. Stone ruins above historic Soldiers' Gulch border one side of the main street, while on the other side are the village's few business establishments. Volcano's residents have eschewed the commercialism of many Gold Rush communities in favor of simple preservation of their historic sites and relics. Most points of interest can be visited on a relaxed walking tour. Attention is focused on Volcano during December, when the town's popular Festival of Lights and Scottish Christmas Walk take place.

The St. George Hotel (circa 1863), a three-story brick building with wooden balconies, is the largest structure in Volcano. It was built in 1863. Visitors can stay in its spartan rooms, which are little changed from the early days; meals are available to guests.

John Austerman

St. Bernard's Catholic Church in Volcano, completed in 1854 and rebuilt in 1931, still serves the community today.

"Old Abe" is a six-pound, 19th-century brass cannon used during the Civil War by the "Volcano Blues" militia and others to intimidate Confederate sympathizers in the area. Housed in a shed just off the main street, it has been used at political rallies and celebrations since the war.

Other Gold Rush relics: *Sieble's Brewery*, a single-story stone structure dating from 1856 . . . the *Old Jail*, whose first prisoners were its builders . . . the *I.O.O.F. and Masonic Hall* (1856), a two-story stone edifice shared by the two orders . . . the *Union Hotel Billiards, Saloon and Boarding House*, rebuilt in 1880 following a fire, now a private residence . . . *Jug and Rose Confectionery*, serving breakfast and lunch in old-fashioned surroundings . . . the *Sing Kee Store*, now a gift and mineral shop, was built in 1854 . . . the *Cobblestone Gallery*, originally erected as a cigar store, now the scene of plays performed by a local theater group . . .*Volcano School*, now a private residence . . . *St. Bernard's Catholic Church*, originally built in 1854 . . . the 1855 stone ruins of the *Clute Building* and the *Kelly and Symonds Emporium* . . . two old cemeteries.

THEN Legend states that the first prospectors to find gold here were soldiers from the New York Volunteer regiment which came to California during the Mexican War. Placer deposits were exceedingly rich, and during 1848 miners averaged over $100 per day per man. Volcano erupted into a boomtown by 1852 when the new Volcano Cutoff road became popular with overland emigrants. When placer mining declined in the mid-1850s and Volcano proved to be outside Amador County's rich quartz belt, local gold-seekers turned to hydraulic mining. Although mining continued into the 20th century, the town was in decline by 1865. Today Volcano lies nearly dormant amid the remnants of livelier days.

JACKSON TO SUTTER CREEK
(4 miles, 8 minutes)

Leaving Jackson, SR 49 climbs a steep hill past a viewpoint above the headframe of the Kennedy Mine, then runs through Martell, a small community dominated by a large lumber mill. The highway then drops sharply into Sutter Creek, offering sweeping views from a hillside overlooking the town.

SUTTER CREEK

NOW Population 2200; elevation 1198 feet. Lodging can be found at several bed and breakfast inns. Restaurants are numerous; other facilities include stores and gasoline stations.

Sutter Creek, nestled in a small valley among rolling hills, is the favorite Mother Lode town of many visitors. It is an attractive community with clean streets, fine homes and many interesting relics of the Gold Rush. The main street is lined with old buildings, many of which sport overhanging balconies; most of these structures are occupied by businesses, including a multitude of antique shops. The residential districts have something of a New England appearance, with many simple, white frame houses. The civic pride of local residents is apparent in the cleanliness and well-kept look of the community and in the historic plaques posted on many of the buildings along the main street. Special events held in Sutter Creek include the Doll and Miniature Show in February, an April Antique Show and Great Duck Race, the Italian Picnic and Parade the first weekend in June, and Currier and Ives Christmas Open House, the first Friday in December.

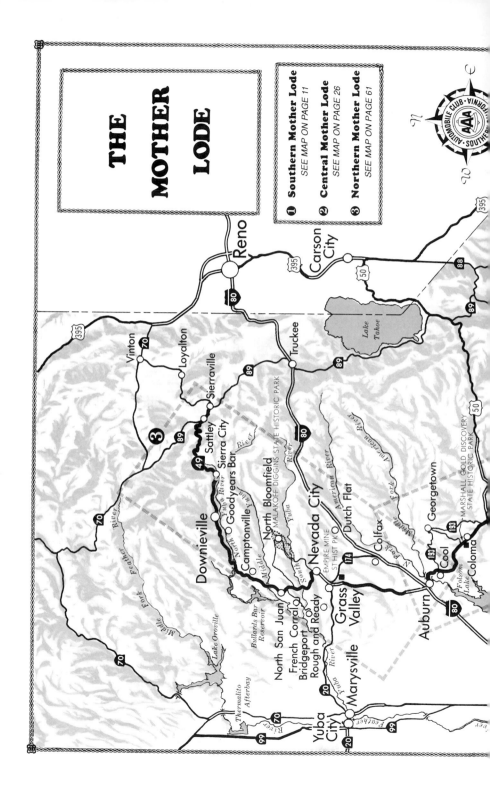

THE MOTHER LODE

① **Southern Mother Lode**
SEE MAP ON PAGE 11

② **Central Mother Lode**
SEE MAP ON PAGE 26

③ **Northern Mother Lode**
SEE MAP ON PAGE 61

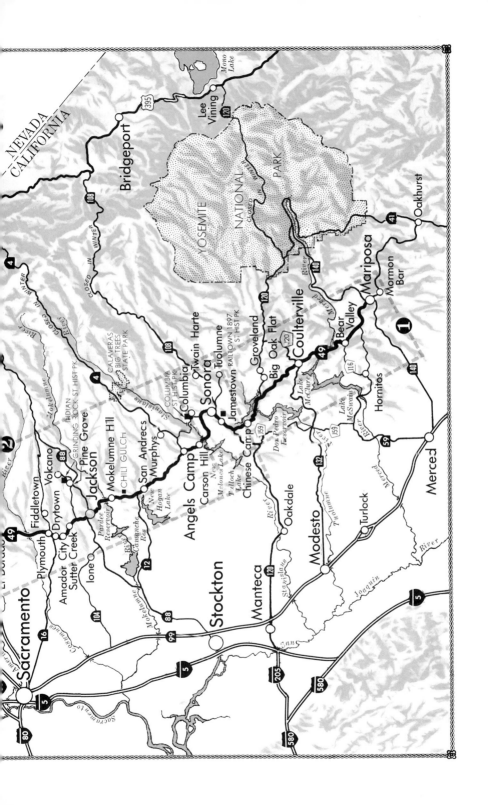

Knight Foundary began operation in 1873, and is believed to be the only water-powered foundary and machine shop still operating in the United States. The facility is located at 81 Eureka St. and is open for self-guided tours daily 9 a.m. to 4 p.m. Adults $2.50; ages 6 to 12 $1.50.

The Methodist Church, built in 1862, sits at the south end of Main St. Its tall, highly visible steeple was not added until 1976.

Sutter Creek Inn was built in 1859 and was at one time the home of State Senator E. C. Voorhies. It has been restored as a New England-style inn, offering bed and breakfast to travelers. Next door is the *Brinn House* (1857), now the Foxes of Sutter Creek Bed and Breakfast Inn.

Immaculate Conception Catholic Church, constructed in 1861, burned down in 1972, but it has been rebuilt as an exact replica of the original. The church is located on Spanish St., west of the business district.

Other points of interest: *Bellotti Inn*, a three-story brick hotel dating from 1867 . . . the *Malatesta Store*, built in 1888 . . . the *Levaggi Building*, which dates from the 1870s . . . the *Downs House* on Spanish St., built in the 1880s for the owner of a local mine . . . the remains of the *Central Eureka Mine*, on a hill just south of town the one-story frame *Monteverde Store*, constructed in 1898 . . . the *Brignole Building* (1865), with its iron doors and shutters . . . the old *Sutter Creek School* (1871), on a slope east of the business district . . . the *I.O.O.F. and Masonic Hall* (1865) . . . *butcher shop* of stone and brick built in the 1870s and 1880s, now a gift shop . . . five fine old homes built in the 1860s and 1870s at the south end of Main St.

Tom Dell

Sutter Creek

THEN Capt. John Sutter established a lumber camp four miles from town around 1845 and later mined for gold using Native American and Hawaiian laborers. Placer gold lasted only a short time around Sutter Creek, but in 1851 rich quartz deposits were discovered. Sutter Creek not only had rich mines, including the Hayward, Central Eureka and the Union (controlled by Leland Stanford). Through the years, nearly $40 million in gold was extracted here from the Central Eureka and other mines, and many tons of gold-bearing ore were crushed in the mills of Sutter Creek. As gold production dropped, lumbering again came into prominence. Today in the county lumbering and government are the chief employers, however, tourism is the bulwark of the town's economy.

SUTTER CREEK TO AMADOR CITY
(2 miles, 3 minutes)

SR 49 climbs out of Sutter Creek, traverses oak-dotted hillsides, then passes the headframe of the Keystone Mine before descending into Amador City.

Bill Escherich

SR 49 forms the main street of tiny Amador City.

AMADOR CITY

NOW Population 202; elevation 954 feet. Limited lodging is available, including a bed and breakfast inn. Facilities consist of several restaurants and a number of antique and specialty shops.

This tiny town with its single-block business district is California's second smallest incorporated city. Several old buildings—some abandoned and some in use—give the village charm, if not size. Most shops close Monday and Tuesday. During the first weekend of December the community celebrates Calico Christmas.

The Mine House was built in 1881 as the headquarters of the Keystone Mine. Today the two-story brick building is a bed and breakfast inn featuring antique furnishings. Each room is named for its original function.

The Keystone Mine was founded in 1853 and produced $24 million in gold, making it one of the richest mines in California. The rusty headframe sits on a hill at the south edge of town.

Also of interest: *The Imperial Hotel* (1879), an imposing two-story brick structure with iron doors and shutters, now reopened as a hotel, bar and restaurant . . . the *Amador Hotel* (1856), currently being restored . . . the *Chichizola General Store*, built in the 1870s, today the post office . . . the *Trading Post*, constructed of rough stone . . . the *Fleehart Building*, which served as the Wells Fargo agency and company store for the Keystone Mine.

THEN Like the county in which it is located, Amador City takes its name from José María Amador, a rancher who mined for gold here in 1848 and 1849. Placer gold was found that year, but it soon gave out. In 1851, however, four ministers-turned-miners discovered rich quartz deposits, and the boom was on. The Keystone Mine, which operated from 1853 until 1942, was one of the greatest producers in the Mother Lode, accounting for some $24 million in gold. Today, without the tourists who stop to look through its shops and historic landmarks, Amador City would be little more than a name in the history books.

AMADOR CITY TO PLYMOUTH
(6 miles, 8 minutes)

Three miles north of Amador City is the village of Drytown, a wide spot in the highway with a small motel, a cafe, several antique shops and a doll store. Founded in 1848, Drytown was once a busy camp with several thousand residents. Not dry at all, the camp at one point boasted as many as 26 saloons, although the exact number is in dispute. The town's name, however, was derived from nearby Dry Creek. Points of interest include the *Butcher Shop*; the *Old General Store*, today an antique shop; and the 1871 *Drytown Schoolhouse*, now the community hall, on a side road east of the highway. Theatrical performances by the "Claypipers" take place weekends May through September. Beyond Drytown, SR 49 runs through rolling hills to Plymouth.

PLYMOUTH

NOW Population 875; elevation 1086 feet. Accommodations, including a bed and breakfast inn, and a campground are available. Facilities include stores and gasoline stations.

A few 19th-century structures stand among newer buildings along the main street, but Plymouth lacks the Gold Rush atmosphere found in most Mother Lode towns. It is a quiet, modest community that serves as a market center for nearby farms and Amador County's growing wine industry. Every July, Plymouth hosts the Amador County Fair.

Points of interest: *I.O.O.F. Hall*, built in 1877 . . . *Ming's Store*, which dates from 1880 . . . the rusting remains of the *Plymouth Consolidated Mine*.

THEN Placer gold provided little wealth here, and water was scarce. But in 1852 a settlement with a store and tavern was established on the stage road between Fiddletown and Sacramento. Quartz deposits, which eventually produced $13 million in gold, spawned additional growth. The town was called Pokerville by local miners, but when the post office was established in 1871, the name was changed to Plymouth, after one of the local mines. This was never known as a boisterous or violent town, and today it remains a peaceful trading center in the heart of the county's vineyard and wine-making region.

♦♦♦

SIDE TRIP TO FIDDLETOWN

Fiddletown is six miles east of Plymouth via a winding road that climbs past farms and ranches through gently rolling countryside. One-way driving time is about 11 minutes.

NOW Population 150; elevation 1687 feet. Facilities include a gas station, a general store, post office and park.

Fiddletown, picturesquely situated in a narrow, wooded valley, is a sleepy but relatively prosperous little community intent on preserving its Gold Rush heritage. Commercialism is almost absent; instead, Fiddletown combines the backwoods atmosphere of a rural hamlet with a genuine 19th-century flavor. Although many of its original structures were destroyed long ago by fire, an interesting group of Gold Rush buildings lines the tree-shaded main street, and homes are scattered along the floor and sides of the valley. In keeping with the town's name, a giant wooden fiddle sits atop the community center.

The Chew Kee Store in Fiddletown is unique among Mother Lode structures in that it is built of rammed earth.

49

Chew Kee Store is a unique building composed of rammed earth, with walls 2½ feet thick. Constructed in 1850, it served as a Chinese herb shop, then as the home of Fiddletown's last Chinese resident, Jimmy Chow, who died in 1965. The store contains many old furnishings and implements. It is open to visitors on Saturday noon to 4 p.m. April through October.

Other historic remains: *The Forge*, originally a blacksmith shop . . . the *Old Chinese Gambling House*, a brick structure dating from the Gold Rush era . . . the *General Store*, in continuous operation since the 1850s . . . the *Schallhorn Building* (1870), formerly a blacksmith and wagon shop . . . the *Purinton House* on Main Street, the oldest residence in town.

THEN Fiddletown purportedly got its name from an elder group of Missourian settlers here who described the younger men as "always fiddlin'." Placer gold provided the impetus for the town's early growth, which resulted in a wild, violent camp composed of tents and shanties, along with a few substantial structures built of wood or stone. When placer mining declined, Fiddletown had established itself as a trading center serving the surrounding mines. Both quartz mining and hydraulic mining were tried here with some success.

Fiddletown's name was changed to Oleta in 1878 at the insistence of the town's people. But a story by Bret Harte entitled "An Episode of Fiddletown" had made the camp's original name unforgettable, and the community was renamed Fiddletown in 1932.

◆◆◆

PLYMOUTH TO PLACERVILLE
(20 miles, 30 minutes)

Five miles north of Plymouth, SR 49 crosses the Cosumnes River and enters El Dorado County. The highway follows the north fork of the river through a thickly wooded canyon for a few miles, then climbs steeply onto a grassy plateau. After passing El Dorado, which began as a mining camp called *Mud Springs*, the highway arrives in Diamond Springs, which in the early 1850s was a thriving Gold Rush community and an important stop on the Carson Emigrant Trail. The old *I.O.O.F. Hall*, built in 1852, and the *Louis LePetit Store* (1856) are remnants of the camp's heyday. Soon after leaving Diamond Springs, SR 49 winds down into Placerville. Facilities along this stretch of the highway consist of several stores and gasoline stations in El Dorado and Diamond Springs.

PLACERVILLE

NOW Population 8355; elevation 1864 feet. Motels, bed and breakfast inns, restaurants, stores and gas stations are plentiful. Other facilities include a hospital, an airport and a California State Automobile Association district office.

One of the most storied of the Mother Lode mining towns, Placerville is today a busy city attempting to recapture some of its colorful Gold Rush heritage. It is the seat of El Dorado County, as well as a trade center for lumbering and agriculture. And thanks to its position at the junction of SR 49 and a major east-west highway (US 50), it is an important stop for travelers.

John Austerman

The Combellack-Blair House in Placerville is an excellent example of Victorian architecture. It is located on Cedar Ravine just south of Main St.

Placerville has in recent years outgrown its historic core, and expansion has taken place well outside the city center, both east and west along US 50. The hub of modern Placerville, however, remains the original downtown area, which is squeezed into a long, slender strip in the bottom of a steep-walled ravine. The single main street is narrow, winding and congested. Although several old buildings still stand here, most have been modernized to house business establishments. The city's past is more evident in the residential districts both north and south of downtown Placerville, where many fine old homes are scattered along pine-clad slopes connected by steep side streets.

Placerville reclaims some of its past with such annual events as the week-long wagon train celebration in June, during which horse-drawn wagons travel down US 50 from Lake Tahoe to Placerville; the El Dorado County Fair, the John M. Studebaker Wheelbarrow Race and the Mother Lode Antique Show in August; the Harvest Fair in September. Information can be obtained at the El Dorado County Chamber of Commerce, 642 Main St.

El Dorado County Historical Museum is located at the fairgrounds west of town, north of US 50. A variety of displays includes a stagecoach, period furniture and replicas of a country store and turn-of-the-century country kitchen. Among the outdoor exhibits are old mining equipment, a replica of a blacksmith shop and a steam locomotive. Open 10 a.m. to 4 p.m. Wednesday through Saturday and 1 to 4 p.m. Sunday in summer; closed Sunday during winter.

Fountain-Tallman City Museum, located on Main St. in what was formerly a soda works, features historical photographs and displays of Placerville's past. Open noon to 4 p.m. Saturday and Sunday.

Gold Bug Mine is the nation's only municipally owned gold mine, and visitors can

51

enter the illuminated mine tunnel. Nearby is an old stamp mill. The mine is located in *Hangtown's Gold Bug Park*, one mile north of downtown Placerville via Bedford Ave. The park is open daily 8:30 a.m. to dusk in summer, until 4:30 p.m. in winter. The mine is open daily 10 a.m. to 4 p.m. May through the first week of October, weekends only rest of October to mid-November and mid-March through April; closed mid-November to mid-March. Self-guided tours are $1 for adults, 50¢ for ages 5-16. For information and reservations for guided tours, call (916) 642-5232.

Methodist Episcopal Church (1851), oldest church in El Dorado County, has been restored and moved to a location on a bluff above Cedar Ravine.

Also of interest: *City Hall*, two buildings that have been joined . . . the ruins of the *Zeisz Brewery*, dating from 1852 . . . *Druids' Monument*, at the corner of Main St. and Cedar Ravine . . . site of the *Hangman's Tree* . . . the *Bell Tower*, which signaled fire alarms . . . the *Combellack-Blair House*, a restored Victorian mansion on Cedar Ravine south of Main St., now a bed and breakfast inn . . . *Nuss Building*, a single-story stone structure erected in 1852 . . . *Masonic Temple*, three stories high, built in 1893 . . . *Episcopal Church of Our Savior*, built in 1865 in the shape of an inverted ship's hull . . . *Pioneers Building*, constructed in 1852 . . . the county's oldest *pipe organ*, with 20-foot-high pipes, on display at the county fairgrounds . . . *Boeger Winery*, dispensing hospitality since the 1870s.

THEN Placerville got an early start, thanks to its proximity to the site of the original gold discovery. In midsummer of 1848, three prospectors took out $17,000 in gold in less than a week, and the rush was on. By 1849 some 4000 miners had staked out every gulch and hillside, and a rip-roaring camp composed of clapboard houses, tents and log cabins sprawled across the landscape. The original name of the camp was *Dry Diggings*, but after becoming the first Gold Rush community to use lynchings as a form of justice, the camp became *Hangtown*.

Not only was the area rich in gold (it produced $25 million in placer gold alone), it was the gateway to the California mines for overland travelers, making it an important supply point. Hangtown quickly became the biggest camp in the Mother Lode. Substantial buildings were erected, and the town acquired many of the accoutrements of civilization. By 1850 it had a church, a temperance society and a theater, along with several fine hotels and restaurants. Since many civic-minded residents felt that Hangtown was an unsuitable name for such a cultured community, the name was changed to Placerville in 1954.

The camp continued to boom, soon becoming California's third largest city. When placer gold became more difficult to find, miners turned to quartz lodes (one mine alone produced $13 million) and eventually to hydraulic mining. A devastating fire in 1856 almost wiped out the town, but Placerville sprang back, this time with more substantial structures of stone and brick. That same year it became the seat of El Dorado County.

Many famous people got their start in Placerville. Railroad magnate Mark Hopkins sold vegetables; Philip Armour, of meat-packing fame, had a butcher shop here;

John Studebaker, who later graduated to automobiles, worked in a wheelbarrow shop; "Snowshoe" Thompson ran a mail route across the Sierra Nevada for many winters; Hank Monk drove overland stagecoaches with celebrated daring and skill; the poet Edwin Markham lived here; and Collis P. Huntington, who later became a railroad tycoon, operated a store in Placerville in 1850.

When many Mother Lode towns began to decline, Placerville continued to prosper—again because of its location. In 1856 a stagecoach negotiated a trail across the Sierra Nevada and back, proving that a regular route was feasible. Soon both overland mail and stage service began, followed in 1860 by the Pony Express. About the same time, news of the rich silver strikes in Nevada's Comstock Lode spread to California, and a reverse rush was on, using Placerville as its chief outfitting point. Tourists now follow the historic routes of the mid-19th century, and Placerville continues to flourish as a stopover.

PLACERVILLE TO COLOMA
(9 miles, 20 minutes)

With its many sharp curves and steep grades, this stretch of SR 49 is one of the slowest on the entire route. After leaving Placerville through a pleasant residential section, the highway reaches the southern junction with SR 193, which leads to Georgetown. SR 49 then winds through hilly countryside punctuated with farms and ranches, descending to Coloma on the South Fork of the American River.

◆◆◆

SIDE TRIP TO GEORGETOWN

The traveler can choose from three routes to Georgetown. Two are formed by SR 193, which branches off SR 49 at the northern edge of Placerville, climbs in and out of the deep canyon of the South Fork of the American River, and crosses forested hills to Georgetown. It then loops westward on a gradual downhill course to rejoin SR 49 at Cool. The third route is Marshall Rd., a county road connecting Coloma with Georgetown. From Placerville, one-way distance is 15 miles; driving time is approximately 25 minutes. The northern leg of the SR 193 loop is 13 miles long and takes about 17 minutes to drive. The Marshall Rd. route, nine miles in length, can be driven in 20 minutes.

NOW Population 3500; elevation 2654 feet. Several lodging establishments can be found, including a bed and breakfast inn, in addition to a neighborhood shopping center with a supermarket, restaurants, gasoline, an airport and basic supplies.

Georgetown, surrounded by pine-covered slopes, is a picturesque mountain town with a Gold Rush background and a number of well-preserved 19th-century buildings in its center. The main street is inordinately wide (100 feet); it was laid out this way as protection against the spread of fire. Georgetown is a quiet, unpretentious village, except in August when it holds its Annual Founders Day Celebration and in July during the three-or four-day Jeepers Jamboree.

53

Balzar House, at the junction of SR 193 and Main St., was originally a three-story building. It was constructed in 1859 for a woman known as the "Widow Balzar," who operated a hotel on the first two floors and a dance hall on the upper story. Business being slow, the building was converted into an opera hall, which also failed. In the 1890s, the top floor was removed, and the structure became the I.O.O.F. Hall.

Tom Dell

The Shannon Knox House, Georgetown's oldest, is on the south side of SR 193.

Shannon Knox House, built in 1864, is the oldest residence in Georgetown. Wood for its construction was shipped to California around Cape Horn—a somewhat ludicrous undertaking, since the house sits within a pine forest.

The Old Armory on Main Street, a small brick building, dates from 1862. It served as an armory during Civil War days and now houses a realtor's office.

Also of interest: *Nevada House Site*, now the rambling *Georgetown Hotel* . . . *Wells Fargo Building and stage stop*, 1852 . . . the *Miners Club*, built in 1862 . . . the 1863 *American Hotel* (now American River Inn), rebuilt in 1899 . . . *Georgetown Library's* brick building constructed in the late 1800s to house two stores . . . *Georgetown Pioneer Cemetery*, established in 1850, just northwest of town along SR 193.

THEN When George Phipps and his party found rich placer diggings here in 1849, they swore the nuggets "growled" in their pans. They named their camp *Growlersburg*, although it was subsequently renamed in honor of its founder. After a fire in 1852 destroyed the camp, it was moved from its original location in Empire Canyon to its present site. In an effort to protect against fire, the town planners rebuilt their community with a main street 100 feet wide and 60-foot-wide side streets; most buildings were constructed of stone and brick. Georgetown was a rich camp that at one time boasted a population of 5000. Deep-shaft mining remained lucrative as late as the 1880s.

COLOMA

NOW Population 186; elevation 750 feet. There is a Victorian-style bed and breakfast inn, along with several restaurants and a campground. Other facilities include stores and picnic areas.

Although Coloma was the birthplace and early focal point of the Gold Rush, today it is a tiny village. Most of the original town site is within the boundaries of Marshall Gold Discovery State Historic Park. Several old buildings line SR 49, but many points of interest lie along the narrow back streets. A brochure can be obtained at the Gold Discovery Museum for 50¢ The park is open 8 a.m. to sunset daily; buildings are open 10 a.m. to 5 p.m. in summer; shorter hours the rest of the year. Day-use fee is $5 per vehicle.

With its pleasant setting and abundance of historic landmarks, Coloma is an enjoyable place to spend a few hours, although the park gets hot and crowded in summer. During the rest of the year, it is usually quiet and peaceful.

Gold Discovery Museum offers an excellent orientation to the park, with instructive exhibits concerning gold and its discovery. Video presentations on the Gold Country are shown on request. (Museum admission and a trail guide are included in the state park day-use fee.)

Sutter's Mill is an exact replica of the mill completed here in 1848, although it is a short distance from the original site (the river has changed course). From the parking lot, marked trails lead to the site where gold was discovered.

James W. Marshall Monument, located on a hill overlooking Coloma and the river, has a statue of Marshall pointing to the spot where he made his gold discovery. Marshall is buried here. The site can be reached by car or via a one-mile hiking trail, beginning at the Gold Discovery Museum.

St. John's Catholic Church dates from 1856. The graceful white frame church, with an old bell in its front yard and a Catholic cemetery in the rear, is located on Church St. near Marshall's cabin.

Other park features: *Emmanuel Episcopal Church*, built in 1856 . . . *Wah Hop Store*, a stone structure containing exhibits depicting its use as a Chinese store during the Gold Rush . . . *Man Lee Store*, with a display of mining artifacts . . . *Bekeart's Gunsmith Shop*, oldest building in Coloma . . . the *Historic Jail*, now in ruins, with its cage-like cells . . . the *Jackson Mill*, a two-stamp crushing mill . . . *Thomas House*, a restored 1860s residence . . . *Marshall's Cabin*, near the Catholic Church . . . the *I.O.O.F. Hall*, built in 1854 . . . *Coloma School*, a one-room schoolhouse currently undergoing restoration . . . *Pioneer Cemetery*, containing many Gold Rush-era graves . . . *Papini House*, built in 1885 . . . *bedrock mortar*, where in pre-Gold Rush days Nisenan Indian women pounded acorns . . . *Vineyard House*, a historic hotel and restaurant, still in operation . . . *Coloma Winery*, built in 1866, a stone ruin behind the Vineyard House . . . *Olde Coloma Theater*, where live melodramas are presented on summer weekend evenings . . . areas for picnicking, gold panning and riverside recreation.

John Austerman

A replica of Sutter's Mill and relics of the Gold Rush line SR 49 in Coloma, the town where gold was first discovered.

THEN Capt. John Sutter needed lumber for his agricultural domain in the Sacramento Valley, so in 1847 he entered into partnership with one of his employees, James W. Marshall, who with a group of Mormon pioneers, agreed to build a sawmill on the South Fork of the American River. On January 24, 1848, Marshall was inspecting the tailrace when he spotted some yellow flecks glistening in the water.

After exhaustive tests, it was determined that the shiny metal was gold. Although Sutter and Marshall agreed to keep the discovery a secret, the news soon leaked out, and the great California Gold Rush was on.

By the summer of 1848, some 2000 miners were feverishly working with shovels and pans along the river, and the first of the Gold Rush towns was born. With the plentitude of lumber in the area, the settlers almost immediately erected substantial frame structures instead of the tents and shanties that characterized most early-day mining camps. By the end of 1849, Coloma had a transient population of 5000, with 13 hotels, two banks, and numerous stores and other businesses. It was here that the limited supply of goods coupled with high demand established prices: shovels and other simple tools cost $50 each, butter was $6 per pound, and shirts that cost $50 were $1 each to have laundered.

Coloma was the first Gold Rush town, but it wasn't the richest. Thousands of miners who came to California looking for gold began their search in Coloma, but most left when news of other rich strikes was heard. Placer gold gave out relatively early here, and by 1851 the town had already begun to decline. By 1856, when the county seat was lost to Placerville, Coloma's fate was sealed. In the years that followed, quartz mining was tried with some success, but Coloma dwindled into a quiet village kept alive by agriculture and mementos of its past.

COLOMA TO AUBURN
(18 miles, 30 minutes)

After climbing steadily past heavily vegetated slopes for eight miles, SR 49 reaches Pilot Hill, site of the magnificent but ill-fated *Bayley House*, a stately structure standing alongside the highway. A.A. Bayley built the three-story mansion in 1862 with hopes of opening a railroad hotel, but the railroad changed its planned route at the last minute, and the building became "Bayley's Folly." Pilot Hill has a store and a gas station, as does Cool, three miles farther up the highway. Past Cool, SR 49 descends into the canyon of the North Fork of the American River. After crossing the river into Placer County, Highway 49 scales the north slope of the canyon and enters Auburn.

AUBURN

NOW Population 11,000; elevation 1255 feet. There are numerous motels and restaurants, as well as several bed and breakfast inns and a campground. Auburn offers the traveler a wide range of services, including a hospital, an airport and a California State Automobile Association district office.

A bustling, sprawling town perched atop a bluff above the North Fork of the American River, Auburn is the metropolis of the Mother Lode. It is a progressive town that prospers without depending on tourism for sustenance. Lumbering is important here, as is agriculture. Auburn is a busy transportation center situated on a transcontinental railroad and a major interstate highway (I-80). It also serves as the seat of Placer County.

John Austerman

The stately Placer County Courthouse overlooks Old Town from its hilltop site.

Despite living vigorously in the present, Auburn takes pride in preserving the remnants of its Gold Rush past. The city long ago outgrew its original site, and most modern development has occurred away from *Old Town*, the historic heart of Auburn. As a result, many old buildings have been left standing. Old Town today is a compact cluster of historic sites and interesting shops, making it an excellent place for a walking tour.

Special events held in Auburn include Wild West Stampede in April, the Annual Flea Market in May, the Auburn District Fair and the Bernhard Museum's Harvest Festival in September, and in December the Festival of Lights Christmas Parade.

Gold Country Museum, 1273 High St. on the Gold Country Fairgrounds, is just south of Old Town. The museum focuses on the Gold Rush and mining history of Placer County. Exhibits include a 48-foot walk-through mine shaft, a working model of a stamp mill, a model dredge, a monitor nozzle used for hydraulic mining, and an assay office. Other exhibits focus on the lives of the forty-niners, and children can try their luck panning for gold. Open 10 a.m. to 4 p.m. Tuesday through Sunday, except holidays. Admission is $1 for adults, 50¢ for ages 6-16 and over 65. Admission includes Bernhard Museum. (916) 889-4134.

The *Bernhard Museum,* located at 291 Auburn-Folsom Rd., near the entrance to the Gold Country Fairgrounds, was built in 1851 as the Traveler's Rest Hotel. In 1868 it became the home of the Benjamin Bernhard family, pioneers in the agricultural and viticultural development of the area. The museum offers guided tours of the home whose furnishings depict life in the late Victorian era. The home is colorfully decorated for Christmas and other special occasions during the year. The museum is open 11 a.m. to 3 p.m. Tuesday through Friday and noon to 4 p.m. Saturday and Sunday, except holidays. Admission is $1 for adults, 50¢ for ages 6-16 and over 65. Admission includes Gold Country Museum. (916) 889-4156.

The Firehouse in Old Town is one of the most photographed old buildings in California. A narrow frame structure with a pointed tower and a colorful red-and-white exterior, it dates from 1891.

The Post Office, a single-story structure with iron doors, was built in 1849. It is California's oldest continuously used post office.

Placer County Courthouse, built in 1894, is one of the finest old courthouses in the western United States. The imposing domed structure sits on a hill overlooking Old Town. Upon completion of extensive restoration now under way, the building will house a museum devoted to the history and development of Placer County.

Pioneer Methodist Church, located near the courthouse, is an attractive frame building dating from 1858.

Other Old Town attractions: The block of old buildings across from the firehouse containing *Lawyers Row, Placer County Bank Building, Masonic Hall* and the *Wells Fargo Office* . . . the statue of *Claude Chana,* who started Auburn's Gold Rush . . . the *Joss House,* still sporting Chinese characters on its facade . . . *Union Bar,* a brick building with a rounded front.

THEN After hearing of James Marshall's gold discovery at Sutter's Mill, Claude Chana organized a party consisting of a few fellow Frenchmen and some two dozen Indians. In May of 1848 they set out from Sutter's Fort for Coloma, making their first night's camp in what is now known as Auburn Ravine. Chana sampled the soil here, found gold, and the party immediately forgot about going on to Coloma. Thus began the camp that bore the names *Dry Diggin's, Wood's Dry Diggin's, North Fork Dry Diggin's* and *Rich Dry Diggin's.* The last name seems most appropriate, since the ravine was generally dry, and it was exceedingly rich. During the first months of the camp's existence, yields of up to $1500 per miner per day were not uncommon. By 1849 the camp had grown into a town with a population of 1500, and miners from Auburn, New York, had renamed it after their home town.

John Austerman

The Firehouse in Auburn makes a good starting point for a leisurely walking tour of the city's Old Town.

Auburn soon became an important trading center and supply depot for the surrounding mines, as well as a stagecoach terminus. It was here that the infamous art of stagecoach robbery was vigorously pursued; the shipment of gold and other valuables was a risky business. In 1852 Auburn won the Sutter County seat, somehow managing to cast a majority vote greater than its entire population. When Placer County was formed the following year, Auburn became its seat. By this time, the town had abandoned its first site in favor of a location farther up the ravine. Nothing remains of the original town; the second stage of Auburn's development took place in what is now Old Town. A disastrous fire swept through the town in 1855, but it was quickly rebuilt— this time with structures of stone and brick instead of log cabins and frame buildings.

During the next 10 years, Auburn's gold supply declined, and the town turned its attention to getting a railroad built here. This quest involved a long, bitter struggle, but in 1856 the Central Pacific finally arrived in Auburn on its way to meet the Union Pacific in Utah. Auburn's position along the first transcontinental railroad ensured the town's future as a transportation center.

Tom Dell

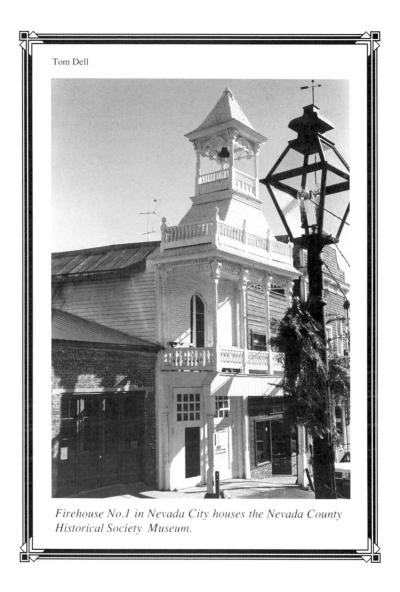

Firehouse No.1 in Nevada City houses the Nevada County Historical Society Museum.

Northern Mother Lode

NOW The northern section of the Mother Lode differs markedly in physical appearance from the southern and central sections. It is characterized by steep, heavily timbered slopes, with pine replacing oak as the most conspicuous tree species. Elevations are higher in this section, varying from 1200 feet near Auburn to 6701 feet at the summit of Yuba Pass. The climate is more seasonal; summers are warm and dry, but winters can bring cold temperatures and occasional heavy snowfall.

THE ROAD Except where it dips into deep river gorges, this 106-mile section of SR 49 climbs steadily through forested hills to the summit of Yuba Pass, then descends into the wide, level Sierra Valley. A few stretches are steep and winding, but driving conditions are generally good. SR 49 remains open all year, although heavy snowfalls can cause temporary closures. SR 20 is the only major east-west highway joining SR 49 north of Auburn; SR 89 leads northwest from Sattley toward Lassen Volcanic National Park and southeast from Sierraville to Lake Tahoe. For more detailed road information, refer to the CSAA *Feather River and Yuba River Regions* map.

FACILITIES Grass Valley and Nevada City offer complete facilities for travelers, but services elsewhere are extremely limited. Campgrounds and trailer spaces are plentiful along the North Yuba River. See the AAA *California/Nevada TourBook* or the California State Automobile Association's *Bed and Breakfast* book for accommodations listings. For camping information refer to the AAA *CampBook* or the ACSC *Central and Southern* and *Northern California Camping* maps.

RECREATION This rugged region offers a wide variety of outdoor activities, including camping, fishing, hunting, gold panning and winter sports.

THEN Placer mining was responsible for the region's early wealth and settlement, but the northern Mother Lode also had some of California's richest and deepest quartz mines. In addition, this was the birthplace of hydraulic mining, and scars from this destructive process still mar many mountainsides. After mining ceased, only Grass Valley and Nevada City continued to prosper; most communities either declined or disappeared.

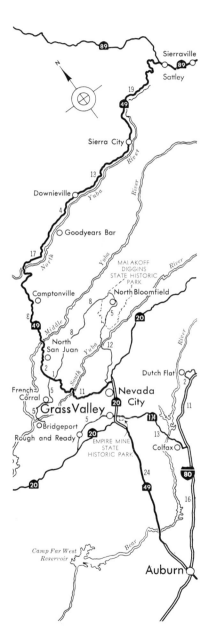

♦♦♦

SIDE TRIP TO DUTCH FLAT

Travelers who leave SR 49 at Auburn and head toward Lake Tahoe or Reno on Interstate 80 can easily visit the charming old mining town of Dutch Flat. The business district is less than two miles off the freeway. It is 29 miles northeast of Auburn; one-way driving time from Auburn is about 35 minutes. Or, since the stretch of SR 49 between Auburn and Grass Valley holds little of historic interest, motorists planning to continue into the northern Mother Lode can take I-80 to Dutch Flat, return on the freeway to Colfax, then proceed directly to Grass Valley via SR 174. The 26 miles from Dutch Flat to Grass Valley can be driven in approximately 35 minutes. Roadside facilities are plentiful along I-80; of special interest is the *Gold Run Rest Area*, just west of Dutch Flat. The rest area features displays of old mining equipment, including a monitor nozzle once used in hydraulic mining.

NOW Population 310; elevation 3144 feet. Facilities in the village consist of a general store, a few shops, library, ice cream and sandwich parlor and a post office. In addition, two restaurants and a delicatessen are located off I-80 at the Dutch Flat exit.

Dutch Flat is a vestige of the 19th century snugly nestled among pine-covered slopes. Despite its proximity to a busy railroad and a modern freeway, this captivating community retains an antique atmosphere. Dutch Flat is one of the few Mother Lode mining camps that never suffered widespread destruction by fire, and many historic buildings are still in use, including a number of frame houses dating from the late 1800s.

The Dutch Flat Hotel is a handsome but well-worn frame structure with overhanging balconies on the second and third stories. The lower floor dates from 1852. About one-third its original size, the building is privately owned and no longer operated as a hotel.

The Methodist Church, on Stockton St. just south of Main St., was built in 1861 and still holds regular services.

Other points of interest: *The General Store*, in business since 1854 . . . *Masonic Hall*, built in 1856 . . . the site of *Strong's Drug Store*, where Dr. D.W. Strong and civil engineer Theodore Judah signed the first subscriptions for the building of the transcontinental railroad . . . the *I.O.O.F. Hall*, an imposing structure erected in 1858 . . . the *Runckel House*, an attractive frame residence in use since 1854 . . . the *Hearse House*, where an antique horse-drawn hearse used in Dutch Flat from 1870 to 1925 is displayed . . . the old *Chinese Store*, an adobe warehouse dating from the 1870s, now restored.

THEN Charles and Joseph Dornbach were merchants who located their store and way station at the present site of the old Dutch Flat School in 1851. Soon a placer-mining camp known as *Dutch Charlie's* sprang into existence. By 1856, when the post office was established, the name had been changed to Dutch Flat. Placer gold provided wealth for many miners in the early 1850s, but the real riches lay beneath the surface, and numerous methods were employed in an effort to get at the gold. Hydraulic mining, begun in 1857, reached its height in the 1860s and continued until 1883, when the practice was outlawed. Dutch Flat was the first mining camp where dynamite was used to uncover gold-bearing gravels. Before the completion of the transcontinental railroad, the town was an important stage stop on the Donner Pass route.

AUBURN TO GRASS VALLEY
(24 miles, 30 minutes)

SR 49 is a busy four-lane highway running through commercial districts for the first few miles after leaving Auburn, but it soon becomes a fast two-lane road that traverses level farming country before climbing into a range of forested hills. Just south of Grass Valley, SR 49 becomes a multi-lane freeway; exits are plainly marked.

GRASS VALLEY

NOW Population 9393; elevation 2420 feet. Accommodations, restaurants are abundant and there are several bed and breakfast establishments. Facilities for travelers are varied and plentiful; they include a hospital, an airfield and a California State Automobile Association district office.

Grass Valley has two personalities that combine to give it a unique character. It is a typical northern mines town with a rich history, several well-kept historic landmarks, pride in its Gold Rush heritage and a happenstance pattern of settlement that follows the irregular contours of the land. At the same time, Grass Valley exudes a tone and life-style as progressive and up-to-date as any community in the gold country.

These two aspects intertwine constantly in the life of the town, occasionally with interesting results. Narrow, congested streets lead onto a modern freeway; a shopping center sits near a pile of old mine tailings; graceful Victorian residences overlook suburban tract homes; and 19th-century buildings of brick and stone contain contemporary stores. Often seeming to be an antique in modern garb, Grass Valley is an old town that "just grew" and is still growing.

It was here that gold mining became a well-organized industry. Many advanced mining techniques were developed and first used in Grass Valley, and the infusion of capital required for efficient exploitation of deep-shaft mines gave the town a broad economic base. Although, agriculture and tourism have replaced gold in the local economy, the sense of organization and efficiency remains. Also recalling the past are many descendants of the Cornish miners who settled here during Grass Valley's mining heyday. Today the city is the scene of a Fourth of July celebration (parade held in Grass Valley in odd years, Nevada City in even years), the Nevada County Fair in August, in September the Draft Horse Classic and Harvest Festival and a Cornish Christmas Celebration every December. For details on Living History Days, Annual Miners Picnic and

Holiday Open House at Bourn ("Empire") Cottage, contact Empire Mine State Historic Park at (916) 273-8522.

John Austerman

The imposing Empire Cottage at Empire Mine State Historic Park was the summer residence of the mine's owner.

Empire Mine State Historic Park, east of SR 49 on E. Empire St., preserves the Empire Mine—one of the oldest and richest gold mines in California. Included in the 800-acre park are the grounds, offices and shops of the mine, the entrance to the mine shaft and the stately stone and brick "Empire Cottage," former summer residence of the mine owner. The park's visitor center and exhibits are open all year. Call for tour schedule; movies and slide shows are presented all year. Visitors are welcome to explore the grounds from 10 a.m. to 5 p.m. daily. Admission is $2 for adults, $1 for ages 6-12, $1 for dogs. The park is located 1 mile east of SR 49 on Empire St. (916) 273-8522.

North Star Powerhouse Mining Museum, located in Boston Ravine (S. Mill St.), is among the finest mining museums in the Mother Lode. Formerly the power station for the North Star Mine, the museum features a huge Pelton waterwheel that was the largest of its type in the world when it was installed in 1896. Other exhibits and displays relate the history and methods of gold mining in the Grass Valley area and the complex process required to refine gold ore. The museum also has on display the largest operational Cornish Pump in the United States. The museum is open 10 a.m. to 5 p.m. daily May through mid-October, depending on weather; call for schedule information during the rest of the year, (916) 273-4255. Admission is by donation.

Lola Montez Home, on Mill St. west of SR 49, is a replica of the house that was built in 1851 and occupied for three years by Lola and her pet bear. It has been furnished with many of Lola's possessions and is now occupied by the Grass Valley Area Chamber of Commerce.

Grass Valley Museum, at S. Church and Chapel sts. in Mount St. Mary's Convent and Orphanage (1863), contains exhibits from the local area, a Victorian parlor and music room, a historic schoolroom, a doctor's office and a rose garden that is more than 100 years old. The museum is open 10 a.m. to 1 p.m. Monday, Tuesday, Thursday and Friday; Wednesday 10 a.m. to 3 p.m.; and June through September noon to 3 p.m. Saturday and Sunday.

Also of interest: *Emmanuel Episcopal Church* on S. Church St., built in 1855 . . . several old brick buildings in the downtown area.

THEN   Good grass, water and timber attracted the first settlers here in 1848, when a sawmill was established. Placer gold was discovered in Boston Ravine soon thereafter, and $4 million was washed in the first five years. But the strike that made Grass Valley famous came in 1850, when George Knight stubbed his toe on a piece of quartz that turned out to contain gold. This event marked the effective beginning of the boom in hardrock mining that kept many Mother Lode camps alive after placer deposits wore thin. Grass Valley went on to become the richest gold-mining town in California, taking out more than $400 million over the years.

When the exotic Lola Montez arrived in 1853 to take up residence, Grass Valley was already a town of 3000. Lola spent two years here, behaving scandalously, entertaining lavishly and encouraging the talents of her young neighbor, Lotta Crabtree. Lola left town in 1855. That same year, Grass Valley suffered what may have been the worst fire that ever hit a Mother Lode camp; 300 frame buildings were destroyed. But the town rebuilt, this time with substantial stone-and-brick structures, many of which still stand in the downtown area.

Mining never let up here, and as a result Grass Valley was one of California's few 19th-century mining towns that never experienced a serious setback. Gold mining became a big business as vast sums of capital, along with the latest in techniques and equipment, were applied to the problems of getting gold out of the earth. One shaft was nearly a mile deep, and the entire town was undermined by a network of shafts and tunnels. The Empire Mine produced more than $100 million, and the Idaho-Maryland and its consolidated mines added $70 million. Not until the mid-20th century did high operating costs force the mines to close.

◆◆◆

SIDE TRIP TO ROUGH AND READY

Rough and Ready lies 4 miles (about 8 minutes) west of Grass Valley on SR 20. Now just a drowsy hamlet with a wedding chapel and a couple of small stores, Rough and Ready once was a busy camp that lived up to its name. Founded by a group of Mexican War veterans, the camp was named in honor of their commanding officer, Gen. Zachary ("Old Rough and Ready") Taylor. Established in 1849, Rough and Ready tried in 1850 to secede from the Union in protest against a mining tax. Great quantities of gold—including an 18-pound nugget—

were found in the area. A few old buildings remain: the *I.O.O.F. Hall*, now a grange hall . . . the weather-worn *Fippin Blacksmith Shop*, where Lotta Crabtree gave her first public performance . . . a second *blacksmith shop* that is now an auto parts and service establishment . . . the *Old Toll House*, now an antique shop.

GRASS VALLEY TO NEVADA CITY
(4 miles, 5 minutes)

For the short distance between these sister cities, SR 49 is a wide freeway. The SR 49/SR 20 Business Route parallels the freeway; one-way driving time via this alternate route is approximately 10 minutes.

NEVADA CITY

NOW Population 2840; elevation 2525 feet. Accommodations are available, including a number of bed and breakfast inns; restaurants are plentiful. Other facilities include stores and gasoline stations.

Many visitors consider Nevada City the most appealing of the major Mother Lode towns. Unlike its bustling sister city, Grass Valley, Nevada City is a peaceful community with a relaxed, dignified atmosphere.

Nevada City is built on steep, pine-clad hills, and its streets follow old miners' trails, coming together in knots and zigzagging across the uneven terrain. This haphazard pattern has been further complicated by the construction of the SR 49 freeway, resulting in many short, dead-end streets.

Norma E. Palmer

Buildings along Nevada City's main thoroughfare, Broad Street, retain a 19th-century appearance.

The appeal of the town lies in its multitude of picturesque Victorian houses, its winding streets lined with sugar maples that come aflame in the fall, its delicate white church spires rising above forested hills, its brick business buildings with gaily painted iron doors and shutters, and its many interesting shops and cafes. This is a town best explored on foot; the Nevada City Chamber of Commerce publishes a brochure outlining a walking tour of the city. (When the Chamber is closed, inquire at the adjoining antique shop.) On a leisurely stroll, the visitor can uncover such unexpected delights as an old-fashioned garden, a window with lace curtains, an inviting park bench, or an out-of-the-way shop specializing in antiques or handicrafts.

Area activities include the Annual Father's Day Bicycle Races in June, Fourth of July Celebration (held in Nevada City in even years, in Grass Valley odd years), Summer Nights the last three Wednesdays in July, and the Constitution Day Celebration and Parade in September. The Annual Artist's Christmas Fair is always held during the three days following Thanksgiving. Victorian Christmas is held three Wednesday evenings and one Sunday afternoon in December.

The National Hotel vies with its namesake in Jackson by claiming to be the oldest continuously operated hotel in California. Begun in 1856 and completed the following year, it is a three-story brick building (painted green) with a long, white balcony. In addition to rooms furnished with antiques, the hotel features a Victorian dining room and a historic tavern.

Nevada Hose Company (Firehouse) No. 1 is a white frame and brick building with intricate "carpenter's lace" on its facade and belfry. The building dates from 1861 and originally housed a fire company; it now contains the Nevada County Historical Society Museum. Open 11 a.m. to 4 p.m. daily April through October; closed Wednesday November through March. (916) 265-5468.

South Yuba Canal Building and Ott's Assay Office, adjoining structures, now house the Nevada City Chamber of Commerce and an antique shop. The canal building was headquarters for a large network of flumes and ditches; the assay office served those bringing silver-bearing ore from the Comstock Lode.

Also of interest: *St. Canice Historical Catholic Cemetery*, on W. Broad St., with many old headstones . . . *First Methodist Church*, a two-story frame edifice built in 1869 . . . *The Red Castle*, a striking Victorian mansion now operated as an inn . . . the *Nevada Theater*, which dates from 1859 . . . the *New York Hotel*, a frame building constructed in 1880 now housing art galleries and specialty shops . . . *Pennsylvania Engine Company (Firehouse) No. 2*, built of red brick with white trim . . . *Searls Historical Library*, containing historical and genealogical research materials.

THEN The first and most famous prospector here was James Marshall, who turned up in 1848 shortly after discovering gold at Coloma. Gold eluded Marshall this time, and he soon departed, leaving the riches of the area to others. In the fall of the same year, a few miners were working rich placers along Deer Creek and had founded a camp of tents and log cabins called *Deer Creek Diggings*. The name was subsequently changed to Caldwell's Upper Store when a merchant opened a branch store here. Placer gold was abundant, but even greater wealth lay in auriferous gravels deposited in an ancient stream bed. In 1850 dozens of "coyote holes" were dug by miners trying to reach the rich gravels, and by the end of the year, a town of 6000 called *Nevada* had arisen. Within another year, the camp had become the seat of newly formed Nevada County.

Fires periodically ravaged Nevada, but after each fire the town was rebuilt. Finally, after the fire of 1856, two effective fire companies were organized, and buildings were constructed of brick, with iron doors and shutters. By this time the population had swelled to 10,000, making this California's third largest city.

As rich as the placers and gravels were, they began to give out in the late 1850s. Then came the news from the assay office that silver ore from the Comstock Lode across the Sierra Nevada was unbelievably rich. By 1859 miners were leaving town as fast as they had arrived a few years earlier. Then in 1864, as an added insult, the new state of Nevada appropriated the name of the town, and mail began to go astray, so the town changed its name to Nevada City. Despite losing most of its inhabitants, Nevada City managed to survive—thanks in part to the continued prosperity of nearby Grass Valley and in part to quartz deposits of its own, which were worked as recently as the early 1940s.

SIDE TRIP TO MALAKOFF DIGGINS STATE HISTORIC PARK

Malakoff Diggins State Historic Park and the old mining town of North Bloomfield lie in heavily forested countryside northeast of Nevada City and can be reached via either of two routes. The Tyler-Foote Crossing road leaves SR 49 approximately 11 miles north of Nevada City. Continue about 15 miles past the Lake City turnoff to the end of the pavement, then follow the signs into North Bloomfield. (Note: after the Lake City turnoff, Tyler-Foote Crossing becomes Cruzon Grade Road.) Total distance to North Bloomfield is 26 miles; one-way driving time in good weather is approximately 50 minutes. An alternate route is North Bloomfield Rd., which leaves SR 49 just west of the junction with SR 20. The first six miles are paved as far as the bridge across the South Yuba River, but beyond the bridge the road is unpaved for approximately seven miles and is narrow, steep and winding—not recommended for trailers and difficult for any vehicle in wet weather. Total distance to North Bloomfield is 16 miles; one-way driving time in good weather is approximately 35 minutes.

Within the park are Malakoff Diggins, the world's largest hydraulic gold mine, and North Bloomfield, the town spawned by the mining operations. At the *Malakoff Pit* (The Diggins), the awesome effects of hydraulic mining are on view; the pit is 7000 feet long and 3000 feet wide, with steeply eroded sides and a shallow lake at the bottom. The pit was nearly 600 feet deep when mining was at its peak, but since that time tons of erosional material have accumulated on the floor, leaving the mine only about 300 feet deep today.

John Austerman

The Malakoff Pit illustrates the ravages of hydraulic mining.

John Austerman

Giant nozzles such as this were used in hydraulic mining to wash away entire mountainsides.

Hydraulic mining was developed in 1853 by Edward Matteson as an efficient way to get at stream-deposited gravels that lie just above bedrock well below the earth's surface. A giant nozzle called a *monitor* unleashed a powerful stream of water that caused the soil on a mountainside to give way. The resulting mud was then directed into a sluice, which caught the heavy gold-bearing gravel; tailings were allowed to

69

flow where they would. Beginning in 1853, a number of small hydraulic operations were at work here, but they lacked the capital necessary for efficient mining. In 1866, a Malakoff miner bought out his partners, rounded up a group of San Francisco investors and founded the North Bloomfield Gravel Mining Company. After acquiring 1500 acres in Malakoff Ravine, the company built an intricate and expensive system of ditches, flumes and reservoirs to bring water for their nozzles. Today this water system carries water to the Grass Valley-Nevada City area.

Hydraulic mining proved to be effective and profitable, but it also wreaked havoc on the environment. Tailings from the mines laid farmlands to waste, silted up the Yuba River until Marysville was under constant threat of flood, and hampered navigation on the Sacramento River and in San Francisco Bay. After a 10-year legal struggle, a law restricting the dumping of mining debris was passed in 1884. This legislation forced the closure of most large-scale hydraulic mining operations. Hydraulic mining continued in California, however, until 1979.

Once a placer camp called *Humbug*, North Bloomfield grew into a busy town of 2000 during the height of hydraulic operations at Malakoff Diggins. Today it is a ghost town that occasionally is used as a movie set. Along its single main street are several restored and preserved buildings, including the *McKillican and Mobley Store*, which during the 1870s and 1880s served as general store, post office and social gathering place.

Park Museum, a former dance hall, features exhibits relating the history of hydraulic mining and life in the area during its peak years; it is open 10 a.m. to 5 p.m. daily in summer, and on some weekends during the rest of the year. Park day-use fee, payable at the museum, is $5 per car, $4 seniors, $1 for dogs. Fee includes parking, hiking, swimming, picnicking, museum and tours.

Also of interest: *St. Columcile's Catholic Church* (1860), which was moved to North Bloomfield from Birchville in 1971 . . . the *Ostrom Livery Stable*, displaying several horse-drawn wagons . . . *Kings Saloon* on the main street . . . a giant *monitor nozzle* near the museum . . . the old *North Bloomfield School*, just west of town . . . several trails near the Malakoff Pit.

The park is open all year, but access roads may be impassable at times during the winter. Five walk-in campsites and three rental cabins are available in addition to a 30-unit campground located just northeast of the North Bloomfield townsite. Camping reservations are recommended during the summer; call MISTIX at (800) 444-7275. The park is seldom crowded, except in June when it hosts its Annual Homecoming Celebration. For information and cabin reservations call (916) 265-2740, 273-3884.

NEVADA CITY TO DOWNIEVILLE

(43 miles, 1 hour)

Beyond Nevada City, SR 49 heads west, then north through heavily forested country-side. After winding smoothly for a few miles, it descends via sharp switchbacks to the South Yuba River, then climbs out of the river canyon and meets a paved side road which leads to the old mining town of French Corral and to Bridgeport, where an antique covered bridge spans the South Yuba River. Just north of the junction is the hamlet of North San Juan. Now little more than a wide place in the road with a small store, cafe and gas station, North San Juan was the scene of busy hydraulic operations during the 1860s. The 1854 *Wells Fargo Building* houses an auto parts store.

After leaving North San Juan, SR 49 dips in and out of the canyon of the Middle Yuba River, then reaches the former hydraulic mining town of Camptonville (store, gasoline station, ranger station), where a monument honors Lester Pelton, inventor of the Pelton waterwheel. After another nine miles, SR 49 drops to the banks of the North Yuba River, where it turns eastward and follows the course of the tumbling river past several campgrounds to Downieville.

DOWNIEVILLE

NOW Population 325; elevation 2865 feet. A limited number of lodging establishments can be found, along with cafes, stores and gasoline stations.

Downieville, seat of Sierra County, is a little mountain community located at the bottom of a picturesque canyon. The town looks much as it must have a century ago, with narrow streets, plank sidewalks, numerous Gold Rush-era buildings of brick and stone, and something of a frontier atmosphere. Several old residences sit precariously on the steep slopes overlooking river and village. In recent years Downieville has experienced a minor "gold rush," with a few modest strikes reported, much to the amusement of the townspeople.

John Austerman

Downieville combines a mountain setting with a Gold Rush flavor.

Downieville Museum is a single-story structure with thick walls of mortarless schist, along with iron doors and shutters; it was originally a Chinese store and gambling house. The building, which dates from 1852, contains interesting relics from Gold Rush days, photographs, household items and clothing from some of the town's pioneer families. A working stamp mill model, handcrafted by local high school boys, is also exhibited. The museum is open 10-5 daily in summer.

Immaculate Conception Catholic Church, an attractive white frame structure, was built in 1858 and is still in use. It is perched atop a knoll north of Main St.

Craycroft Building was originally a log saloon with a 70-foot-long bar. In the early 1850s, the two-story brick building housed, among other things, a newspaper office and a jail; it now shelters a grocery store.

The Hirschfeldter Building, built in 1852, has schist walls four feet thick at the base. It is now a grocery store; the sidewalk in front of the store is made of wooden planks.

United Methodist Church, organized in 1855, is California's oldest Protestant church still in use. The church is located on SR 49 just south of the Downie River.

Also of interest: The *I.O.O.F.-N.D.G.W.* and *Masonic Hall* buildings, built in 1864 . . . the stone office of the *Mountain Messenger*, a newspaper first published in 1853 and still in operation . . . the *Gallows*, built in 1885 for a single hanging . . . the site of *Major Downie's Cabin* . . . the *Downieville Foundry and Machine Shop*, which dates from 1855 . . . *Downieville Heritage Park*, providing picnic tables amid old mining equipment.

THEN   After gold was discovered along the lower Yuba River, Maj. William Downie took a small party up the canyon of the north fork. In the late fall of 1849, the group camped at a spot where the river forked. Prospecting revealed rich placer deposits, and the site, which became known as *The Forks*, developed into a busy, brawling camp. During the first year of the camp's existence, it was rumored that a tin cup could be filled with gold daily. Perhaps because of this, within a year the camp had a population of 5000; it was soon renamed in honor of its founder. So many miners were working the banks of the North Yuba that it was said that a message could be transmitted by word of mouth from Downieville to Marysville in 15 minutes.

The wealth didn't come easy. Miners had to earn their gold by working long, tedious hours in icy, swirling water. Most slept on the ground and subsisted on salt pork and beans. All supplies had to be brought in over a trail that was nearly impassable. As a result, necessities were both scarce and expensive: a wool shirt cost $50, and potatoes were $3 per pound. Later, after the trail was improved, pack trains began bringing in a variety of supplies. Diversion for the miners was provided by saloons that featured every type of elegant appointment except mirrors—the trail was still too rough to transport them.

Downieville wasn't a terribly wild town, but one incident made it infamous throughout California. In 1851, a beautiful dance-hall girl named Juanita stabbed a miner to death. Whether or not she acted in self-defense is still debated, but after a quick trial and a trip to a hastily erected gallows, Juanita became the first woman to be hanged in California. News of her hanging so appalled the state's populace that lynchings became rare thereafter.

DOWNIEVILLE TO SIERRA CITY
(13 miles, 20 minutes)

SR 49 continues to wind up the narrow canyon of the North Yuba River, which in spring and early summer is usually a torrent. The gradient is steeper in this stretch as the highway gains an average of 100 feet per mile. Scattered here and there on the forested mountainsides are a few ramshackle miners' cabins.

SIERRA CITY

NOW Population 225; elevation 4187 feet. Accommodations and restaurants are available but limited; there are two bed and breakfast inns. There is one campground in town and several located along SR 49 both east and west of town. Facilities include cafes, stores and gasoline stations.

Strung out along the north bank of the Yuba River, Sierra City is dwarfed by the massive, austere Sierra Buttes. The village combines the setting of a mountain resort with the flavor of the Gold Rush. A few well-worn buildings, some over 100 years old, line the main street, while some interesting old residences can be found along the narrow back streets. A map brochure outlining points of interest in the area is available at several local businesses.

Sierra County Historical Park and Museum, one mile east of Sierra City on SR 49, is located at the Kentucky Mine, a hard-rock gold mine dating from the 1850s and last worked in 1953. The museum contains displays depicting early life in Sierra County and includes local minerals and wildflowers, Chinese immigrant and Maidu Native American artifacts, and logging and mining equipment. Also, guided tours are offered of the mine's operable 10-stamp quartz mill. The park and museum, operated by the Sierra County Historical Society, are open and tours are offered 10 a.m. to 5 p.m. Wednesday through Sunday, Memorial Day through September; weekends only in October, weather permitting. Museum admission is $1, tours (including museum admission) are $4; children under 12 free when accompanied by an adult. Picnic facilities are available. A concert series is held in the park's amphitheater on Friday evenings during July and early August. (916) 862-1310.

Other points of interest: The *Busch Building*, an impressive brick structure with iron doors and shutters; dating from the 1870s, it once served as the *Wells Fargo office* and is now a bed and breakfast inn . . . *Masonic Hall*, built in 1863 . . . the *Zerloff Hotel*, built in 1885 . . . the *Cemetery*, founded in the 1850s . . . many residences over 100 years old.

THEN Sierra City first developed as a trading center, but in the 1850s gold was discovered here. The Sierra Buttes Mine, north of town, became the greatest producer in the upper reaches of the North Yuba River. Altogether the district took out more than $300 million in gold, including a 141-pound nugget in 1869.

SIERRA CITY TO SIERRAVILLE
(22 miles, 35 minutes)

East of Sierra City, SR 49 continues to climb up the canyon of the North Yuba River. A few miles east of town is the junction with Gold Lake Rd., which leads to several high-country lakes known for excellent fishing. The junction marks the site of the *Bassett House*, an important stage and freight stop between 1871 and 1906. Past the Gold Lake junction, SR 49 winds to the 6701-foot summit of Yuba Pass, then drops quickly via switchback curves to the floor of the wide, level Sierra Valley. At Sattley, SR 89 branches off to the northwest, leading to Quincy, the Feather River canyon and Lassen Volcanic National Park. Sierraville, five miles farther east, marks the second junction with SR 89, which winds southeast to Truckee and Lake Tahoe. SR 49 continues for another 25 miles to Vinton, where it ends at a junction with SR 70.

Personalities of the Mother Lode

California's Gold Rush era was one of the most exciting periods in western history. The scramble for instant wealth provided most of the excitement, but a good deal of the Mother Lode's flavor derived from the facts and legends surrounding some of the colorful characters who roamed the gold fields. This section contains brief biographical descriptions of a few of the most interesting personalities who left their mark on the gold country.

BLACK BART

The infamous robber Black Bart got his name from his habit of leaving bits of poetry, which were signed "Black Bart– PO-8" (poet), at the scene of a robbery. Although he got off to a late start, he engineered 28 Wells Fargo stagecoach robberies before his arrest.

In each robbery, his method was the same. He waited along the trail at a narrow or uphill spot that required the horses to slow down, then stepped into the road as the stage approached. Holding a shotgun in his hand, he said quietly, "Would you throw down your treasure box, sir?" His face was covered by a flour sack, with holes cut for eyes. His impeccable suit was covered by a long linen duster. Over his shoulder Bart slung a blanket roll containing an axe for breaking open the box. The gun used was later found not to contain any shells.

Black Bart always committed his robberies alone, disdaining even the assistance of a horse. He would walk to the scene of the crime, then disappear on foot with the treasure rolled in his blanket. Occasionally he would make dummies, arm them with broomsticks and lodge them in rocks along the road—thus giving the appearance that he had accomplices covering the stagecoach crew. His manner was mild—some said even polite. He took only the box and never bothered the passengers, earning himself the title "Robin Hood of the West."

Ironically, a passenger was responsible for Bart's capture in 1883. Just before Bart's 29th attempt, a passenger had been let off the coach to do a little hunting. After the robbery, the driver returned to where he had let the hunter out. With the armed passenger, the driver returned to the scene of the robbery and surprised Bart in the process of chopping open the box. Bart escaped but left a handkerchief.

A laundry mark (FX07) on the handkerchief enabled police to trace the villain through a San Francisco laundry. The police made one of the most surprising arrests in history, when Black Bart turned out to be Charles E. Bolton, a respected San Francisco citizen.

Bolton was born Charles Boles in Illinois. After serving as a sergeant in the Union Army, he came west to find gold. Unable to find any by legal means, he resorted to other methods.

Boles worked as a clerk for several stage lines, learning the schedules and shipments. Armed with his knowledge and an empty shotgun, he committed his first holdup sometime after 1875 (historians disagree about the exact date).

After a trial in San Andreas during which he pleaded guilty, Boles was sentenced to six years in San Quentin Penitentiary. He served the sentence and, with time off for good behavior, returned to San Francisco. Boles later moved to the San Joaquin Valley, where he quietly dropped out of sight.

A rumor circulated that Wells Fargo gave him a pension in exchange for a promise not to turn again to robbery, but the story was never verified. He disappeared as quietly from history as he had appeared.

LOTTA CRABTREE

When she was six years old, Lotta Crabtree made her first public appearance dancing before a cheering crowd at a smithy in Rough and Ready. Her mother had recognized her precocious talents and saw to it that Lotta was tutored and launched on a tour of the gold fields. Dancing and singing, Lotta charmed the miners with patriotic songs, jigs, impersonations and skits. She was an instant sensation. For years Lotta toured the camps, accepting coins, gold nuggets and other gifts from the appreciative miners. She evidently reminded them of their families and the children they had left behind. Later she captivated the citizens of San Francisco and traveled to New York. Lotta retired at an early age and lived happily until her death (1924) at the age of 77. Her estate totaled more than $4 million.

ELANOR DUMONT

Elanor Dumont captured the heart of Nevada City in 1854 from the moment she stepped from the Concord coach into the dusty streets. The town was shocked when she opened a gambling parlor—a woman gambler was unheard of. But her personal charm was so great that everyone forgave her, even the losers. In Nevada City she acquired the nickname of "Madame Moustache" because of a downy growth on her upper lip.

She lost her heart only once. At age 38 she met and married a small-time promoter, who soon spent her money and deserted her. From that day on luck also deserted Madame Moustache. She moved often, working in successively smaller, more dismal places, until near the end she had to hire girls to entice men to her games. On September 9, 1879, living on borrowed money in Bodie, she took her life.

BRET HARTE

Bret Harte came to San Francisco in 1854 at the age of 18 to be with his mother, who had remarried after Bret's father died. Restless and looking for adventure, Harte headed for the Mother Lode. For a time he taught school in La Grange, then half-heartedly worked as a miner near the Stanislaus River and Angels Camp. In due course he wound up at Jackass Hill, where friends gave him stage fare back to San Francisco.

Bret Harte never really absorbed a detailed knowledge of mining nor found a real identification with the miners. He always stood out as a city slicker, wearing high collars and boiled shirts. He admitted from the start that he couldn't stand the rough camps, hated the hard work, and once wrote that the Sierra region was "hard, ugly, unwashed, vulgar and lawless."

But for all this, his stories had an authentic flavor that portrayed life in the mines as it truly was. In 1860 he published *M'liss*, his first mining story, and from that day on his tales were best-sellers. He never returned to the gold fields, going first to San Francisco, where he enjoyed a successful editorial career, then later to the East Coast and eventually to England. But his writing was always concerned with the frontier and the mines.

JAMES MARSHALL

James Wilson Marshall was born in New Jersey in 1810. As a young man he moved to Missouri, where he worked as a farmer and carpenter, but ill health forced him to move to a better climate. He chose California.

In 1847 Marshall entered into partnership with Capt. John Sutter to build a sawmill. After much searching, a site in Coloma, some 45 miles above Sutter's Fort, was selected for the mill's construction. John Bidwell, an employee of Sutter, later wrote, "Surely no other man than Marshall ever entertained so wild a scheme as that of rafting sawed lumber down the canyons of the American River, and no other man than Sutter would have been so confiding and credulous as to patronize him." Under the agreement, Sutter was to obtain the provisions, tools and teams, while Marshall was to build and run the mill. Marshall was only 37 when he entered into this partnership, but he seemed much older because of his beard, his eccentric personality and his position as foreman. Sutter was only seven years older.

On the morning of January 24, 1848, while inspecting the tailrace, Marshall discovered flakes of gold. Later, while describing it to a fellow miner, Marshall exclaimed, "I reached my hand down and picked it up; it made my heart thump, for I was certain it was gold." He later took the samples of gold to Sutter, who, after much testing, determined it was pure. Although both tried to keep the discovery secret, word leaked out—and the miners poured in.

For a time Sutter and Marshall tried to claim ownership of the area around Coloma, and Marshall attempted to charge a commission for the gold mined there. Most miners just laughed at his efforts and, when he persisted, drove him off the land.

Some time later Marshall started to claim supernatural powers which enabled him to find gold. His claims attracted miners who pressured him to divulge his secrets; when he refused, they threatened to lynch him, and he had to flee for his life. Marshall then tried to prospect in the area, but his face was so well known that he gathered followers wherever he went. As he had to make a living somehow, Marshall returned to Coloma and began to grow a vineyard; he helped develop some mines around Kentucky Flat; he went on a lecture tour and sold autographed pictures of himself; and he operated a blacksmith shop in Kelsey

Marshall died in 1885 at age 74. He was buried on a hill overlooking the site where he first discovered gold. Although he was not penniless when he died, fate did not allow him the wealth he discovered for others.

LOLA MONTEZ

 Lola Montez was born Eliza Gilbert in Ireland. She came to the Mother Lode from Europe, where she had been a sensation because of her theatrical talents and personal life. Lola had been the mistress of Ludwig of Bavaria and the center of attention for the foremost literary and artistic figures of the day: Franz Lizst, Victor Hugo, Alexander Dumas and George Sand were her intimate friends. She loved to be referred to as the Countess of Lansfeldt, a meaningless title given to her by one of her former lovers. She toured the United States, packing houses wherever she went.

Lola charmed San Francisco audiences with her famous Spider Dance, in which spiders made of cork were shaken out of her dress. She moved on to Grass Valley and quickly became the center of the social whirl. Here she lived the good life, giving big parties and enjoying a life-style that included a monkey and a grizzly bear for pets. Despite the frantic whirl, Lola tired of Grass Valley and went on tour to Australia. The trip was a failure, so she turned to a lecture tour in the United States—and flopped again. When her health failed, Lola went to New York, where she spent her last few years in quiet seclusion. She died at age 43.

JOAQUIN MURIETA

Separating fact from fable about Joaquin Murieta gives the student of history as much difficulty as separating gold from gravel gave the miner. Hardly a city in the Mother Lode is without its tales of the adventures of a bandit named "Joaquin." All claim the bandit was Joaquin Murieta; the tales are reinforced by such relics as tunnels alleged to be his escape routes or saloons said to be his favorite drinking spots.

Joaquin Murieta arrived from Sonora, Mexico, in 1850. In the town of Murphys, so the story goes, Yankee persecutors tied him to a tree, beat him, assaulted his wife and murdered his brother. Murieta swore he would get revenge, and from that day he led a life of crime and rampage against the miners.

He is said to have robbed the miners by day, then slipped into towns at night to find pleasure in the saloons and cantinas. Newspapers of that era do, in fact, list the exploits of a bandit named Murieta, but the accounts cover only a two-month period.

In 1853 the California legislature hired Harry Love, a former Texas ranger, to hunt Murieta down. He was paid $150 a month and had a chance at a $5000 reward. Surrounding himself with the toughest crew available, Love rode off from Quartzburg after the elusive bandido. He finally caught up with him, slaying the desperado after a ferocious gunfight.

Love cut off Joaquin's head and the hand of "Three-Fingered Jack," Joaquin's lieutenant, and returned to claim his reward—with the grisly remains pickled in alcohol. There is some doubt about whether the head was truly that of the bandit "Joaquin"; Harry Love may also have made up the name "Murieta."

The lightning raids Joaquin had made, the strong emotion that motivated his desire for revenge, and his Robin Hood-like qualities soon captured the imagination of historians and writers. A writer named John Rollins Ridge wrote *The Life and Adventures of Joaquin Murieta, the Celebrated California Bandit*. Many other writers soon followed suit, each time embellishing the story, until Murieta emerged brave, handsome, romantic and a hero of the people. Many writers visited the area, each adding to the store of "information" and claiming to have received the "evidence" for his book from some personal friend of the dead bandit. Portraits were painted by artists claiming to have seen him. Even Hollywood eventually got into the act, basing a movie on his life.

JOHN SUTTER

Instead of bringing wealth to John Augustus Sutter, the discovery of gold dealt the final blow to his precariously erected empire.

Sutter was born in Switzerland in 1803. Before age 30 he had married, fathered a family, and built up such a tremendous list of business debts that he had to flee to the United States to escape debtors' prison. He eventually arrived in California, via Oregon, Alaska and Hawaii, with a retinue of followers—including Hawaiians, American Indians and a couple of mistresses. Sutter was granted 50,000 acres of land at the confluence of the Sacramento and American Rivers by the Mexican governor of California. His personal charm enabled him to convince the governor that he was a man of great importance.

Sutter, with the help of neighboring Indians, cleared the land and built a town called New Helvetia (New Switzerland). This was the beginning of what is now Sacramento. He ruled the town as if it were his own kingdom. The Indians were his subjects, and his fort, complete with guns and uniformed sentries, was his castle. He was able to build shops, grow crops, raise cattle and conduct a lively trade on his grant of land. New Helvetia became an important stopover for settlers arriving in California in the early 1840s.

In 1841 the Russians sold Fort Ross on Bodega Bay to Sutter on credit, further expanding his empire. Although it was a shaky structure at best, he managed to hold it together by mortgaging his property and forging an occasional check. He was known as a kind and hospitable man, and everyone was welcomed at New Helvetia. Sutter bought all the goods he could with as much as he could pay, but this practice quickly got him into debt. It is estimated that his debt to the Russians alone amounted to nearly $100,000. His kindness and generosity were also detriments. Sutter, who hired anyone wanting employment, was robbed by many a man in his employ.

After gold was discovered, he became a strong proponent for statehood, hoping to prevent squatters from taking New Helvetia. Eventually all his workers deserted to seek gold; the Russians foreclosed on his debt; the court refused to honor his claim to the gold-rich land around Coloma, where his sawmill stood; and the squatters carved up new Helvetia, as he was powerless to drive them out. For a while he was able to slow the rush to ruin by renting the fort buildings to merchants, who were doing a good trade in food, clothing and mining supplies. Reasoning that all miners needed these essentials, Sutter opened stores at Coloma and Sutterville. Because he couldn't operate them by himself, he hired partners who seemed trustworthy. He then bought supplies at high prices from fort merchants. Wagon loads of these goods were shipped out almost daily, but unfortunately, the gold from their sale failed to reach Sutter's coffers.

News of Sutter's financial bind reached Europe, and one of his sons came to California to attempt to create a semblance of order. Sutter left his son to face the indignant creditors and, taking what money he had, went on a wild spree. When he returned, the son had salvaged part of the funds; but Sutter again took control of the estate and, after one brief period of prosperity, left for another spree. His affairs were never put in order again.

At age 66, Sutter left California for Washington, D.C., to try to get a reimbursement from the federal government for the losses he suffered in giving aid to California-bound emigrants, and for the land and money he lost because of the gold discovery. For 11 years he personally pleaded his case with important government officials, but he was never successful. Sutter died almost penniless on June 18, 1880.

MARK TWAIN

Samuel Clemens came west in 1861. After working as a river-boat pilot, printer, newspaperman and even a Confederate soldier for a very short period, he accompanied his brother, Orion, when the latter reported for his new position as governor of the Nevada Territory.

For a time Clemens tried his hand at mining in Nevada and California, but gave it up gladly to take a job as a reporter on the *Virginia City Enterprise*. There he began using the name that recalled his days on the Mississippi—Mark Twain. Twain had an irrepressible sense of humor and an urge to travel. The latter propelled him to San Francisco, and the former resulted in his banishment from the city when his writings rubbed the police chief the wrong way.

Mark Twain visited some friends near Angels Camp in 1864. A man told him a funny story about a frog-jumping contest that was lost when someone fed buckshot to one of the famed leapers. This tale became the basis for "The Celebrated Jumping Frog of Calaveras County." When his version was printed in an eastern magazine, Mark Twain became an immediate sensation. A year later he left California, but he carried with him a wealth of impressions that influenced his writings for the rest of his life.

Glossary

The following is a partial list of the words and terms that were most commonly used in the Mother Lode country during the Gold Rush. A better understanding of them will add more pleasure to your trip. It should be understood that the explanations and definitions presented here are very general and that variations will occur in some sections of the Mother Lode.

Amalgamation A process by which gold is separated from ore. The ore is crushed in a mercury-water solution and subjected to violent agitation. This motion breaks up the mercury into minute particles which adhere to the gold. Later, when the gold has partially separated from the mercury, the remaining mass is heated in a retort. The mercury leaves in the form of a vapor, which is condensed and used again. The gold is now almost pure and is cast into bars.

Argonauts A term referring to the adventurous gold-seeking men of '49 who came to California in their search for the precious yellow metal.

Arrastra A primitive, mule-powered device for crushing ore. An arrastra was a shallow, circular pit with a sturdy rotating post set in the center to which heavy beams were attached. The beams were in turn hooked to large blocks of stone. Ore was dumped into the arrastra and mixed with water. Mules were used to rotate the apparatus, reducing the ore to a muddy mass. The gold could then be separated by panning or amalgamation.

Assay Office A place where an expert will assay, or evaluate, the mineral content of any ore by a chemical analysis.

Bar Referring to rivers; generally, a bank of sand, gravel or rock. The word was used in the name of any camp that happened to spring up along a river bar, such as Mormon Bar, Goodyears Bar, Bidwell Bar, Douglas Bar, etc. There were dozens of these camps, most of which were flooded out during storms (the bars were usually worked at times of low water).

Bullion Gold or silver that has not been minted, usually stored in the shape of bricks or bars.

Diggings A term used by many of the early-day miners when referring to a claim or region that was being worked or mined for gold.

Dredging This process consists of a barge or boat equipped with machinery that scoops the gold-bearing gravel from the river beds. The gravel is then processed by washing or sluicing. Although this process was rarely used in the Mother Lode, it was used extensively on the rivers of the upper San Joaquin and Sacramento Valleys.

Dust A term used to describe minute particles of gold taken from the placers. This "dust" was used as money. In many of the camps, a dollar in dust was the amount that could be held between the thumb and forefinger. This was called a "pinch." A whiskey glass was used to measure $100.

Fandango Halls These halls sprang up in the camps where great numbers of Mexican miners lived, such as Hornitos. They were named for the famous "fandango," a lively dance performed by señoritas to the accompaniment of guitars and castanets.

Flume An inclined channel, usually constructed of wood or stone, used to convey water for long distances. Sometimes flume also refers to a narrow gorge or ravine used for the same purpose.

Glory Hole A hole producing extraordinary amounts of gold. Mining procedures varied, but usually consisted of sinking a vertical shaft to the bottom of the pay-ore, then connecting it with a horizontal tunnel. The top of the shaft was broken out, forming a funnel. The ore slid to the bottom, where it was loaded into cars and hauled away.

Hardrock (Quartz) Mining This is an underground method of mining, started in 1850 after George Knight discovered the first gold-bearing quartz near Grass Valley. It is a very expensive method and is accomplished by sinking a shaft over the vein or pocket of ore, with drifts, or tunnels, running out from various levels. One of the largest quartz mines attained a vertical depth of 5912 feet, with several miles of drift. Tremendous investments were necessary in addition to the labor expense in sinking the shaft: stamp mills had to be built, tanks had to be constructed to store the chemicals used in the process, and equipment was needed to raise the ore from such depths.

Hydraulic Mining This method of mining consisted of concentrating powerful jets of water upon a specific area and washing the gold-bearing earth or gravel into a sluice. Ridges in the bottom of the sluice saved the "dust" and allowed the mountains of earth to pass into the creeks and rivers. The dirt eventually caused a navigation hazard in major rivers and San Francisco Bay, which led to legislation that eventually brought an end to hydraulic mining.

I.O.O F. Initials stand for the Independent Order of Odd Fellows, a fraternal organization founded in 1819.

Joss House A Chinese house or temple used as a place of worship.

Monitor The name given the huge nozzles used in hydraulic mining that shot jets of water, washing away whole mountainsides in the search for gold

Nugget A lump of native gold of no special size, but usually bigger than the head of a match. The largest nugget ever found in the Mother Lode weighed 195 pounds.

Panning A method of extracting gold from stream beds. A saucer-shaped pan is partially filled with gravel and dipped in water. The pan is then moved gently in a circular motion to wash out the lighter gravel. The gold, being heavier, sinks to the bottom and remains.

Placer Claim Any mining claim that has been located, or "staked out," over a mineral deposit. These placer deposits were built up over the ages through the erosion process, which is why most claims were located along rivers, creeks and dry stream beds.

Placer Mining The process of gathering the precious metals from a placer claim. This was accomplished by several different methods, including panning, hydraulic mining, dredging and sluicing. Because of the importance of water in all of these processes, the placer claim was usually located on or as near as possible to a stream. In many instances rich placer claims were located high and dry, and water was brought in by flume and ditch to complete the process.

Pocket A mining term referring to a small but rich concentration of gold in a quartz vein. This term, applied to placer mining, generally means a low spot or hole in a stream bed that has captured the dust and nuggets.

Poke A crude leather pouch equipped with a drawstring. It was used by the miners to store or carry dust and nuggets.

Quartz A very common, hard mineral, often found in crystal formations but generally found in large masses or veins. Many semiprecious stones are forms of quartz; however, the quartz that was mined in the Mother Lode was excavated for its gold content. (See "Hardrock Mining.")

Retort A furnace used to heat a mixture of gold and mercury. The mercury is passed off in a vapor and saved; the gold is then formed into bars.

Rocker A crude machine used mainly by the Chinese in working the placers. This contraption consisted of a sieve-bottomed hopper mounted on a rocker. Water and earth were fed into the hopper as the machine was rocked. The rocking motion washed the earth through the sieve onto a slanting apron. Ridges lining the bottom of the apron trapped the gold and allowed the lighter gravel and earth to be washed out.

Sluicing This method of extracting gold from the rich placer claims consisted of a long inclined series of troughs (sluice boxes) to which riffles or slats were fixed across the bottom. Gold-bearing earth or gravel and water were fed into the sluice at the upper end. The water was regulated to carry the earth over the riffles and out, allowing the heavier gold to settle and be trapped by the riffles. Quicksilver (mercury) was sometimes placed behind the riffles to catch the gold.

Sniper The name given to a person who prospects over old "diggings" looking for gold.

Stamp Mill A mill that breaks and grinds the gold-bearing ore, saving the gold by means of amalgamation.

Strike A term applied to the discovery of a new concentration of gold rich enough to be mined profitably.

Tailings The waste left after gold-bearing ore or gravel has been processed.

Tailings Wheels The huge wheels, sometimes 50 feet in diameter, used to transport tailings from the mill to a dump. The dump was usually located away from the mill to prevent the ever-growing mountains of waste from cluttering up and isolating the mill site.

Worked Out An expression used when referring to a claim, mine or area that has been thoroughly mined of all the gold that is profitable to mine.

Mother Lode Chambers of Commerce

The following list of chambers of commerce is provided to enable members to obtain more complete information about the Mother Lode country and what it has to offer.

Amador County
P.O. Box 596
125-B Peek St.
Jackson 95642
(209) 223-0350

Auburn Area
601 Lincoln Wy.
Auburn 95603
(916) 885-5616

Calaveras County
Visitor Information Center
P.O. Box 637
Angels Camp 95222
(209) 736-0049
(800) 225-3764

El Dorado County
542 Main St.
Placerville 95667
(916) 621-5885

**Grass Valley and
Nevada County**
248 Mill St.
Grass Valley 95945
(916) 273-4667

Mariposa County
P.O. Box 425
5158 N. Hwy 140
Mariposa 95338
(209) 966-2456

Nevada City
132 Main St.
Nevada City 95959
(916) 265-2692

North Mariposa County
P.O. Box 333
5009-B Main St.
Coulterville 95311
(209) 878-3074

Tuolumne County
55 Stockton St.
Sonora 95370
(209) 532-4212

California State Automobile Association District Offices

The California State Automobile Association district offices listed below are located in or near the Mother Lode area.

Angels Camp
451 S. Main St.
(209) 736-4517

Auburn
2495 Bell Rd.
(916) 885-6561

Carson City
2901 S. Carson St.
(702) 883-2470

Grass Valley
113-B Dorsey Dr.
(916) 272-9011

Jackson
2092 W. SR 88
(209) 223-2761

Lake Tahoe
961 Emerald Bay Rd.
(SR 89)
South Lake Tahoe
(916) 541-4434

7717 N. Lake Bl.
Kings Beach
(916) 546-4245

Lodi
1335 S. Fairmont Av.
(209) 334-9671

Manteca
145 Trevino Av.
(209) 239-1252

Marysville
1205 D. St.
(916) 742-5531

Merced
3065 M St.
(209) 723-9143

Modesto
3525 Coffee Rd.
(209) 523-9171

Oroville
1430 Feather River Bl.
(916) 533-3931

Placerville
1323 Broadway
(916) 622-4084

Reno
199 E. Moana Ln.
(702) 826-8800

Roseville
2100 Professional Dr.
(916) 784-3232

Sacramento
4333 Florin Rd.
(916) 422-6511

4745 Chippendale Dr.
(916) 331-7610

15 Bicentennial Cr.
(916) 381-3355

Sonora
301 S. Shepherd St.
(209) 532-3134

Stockton
49 W. Yokuts Av.
(209) 952-4100

Turlock
2160 Geer Rd.
(209) 668-2722

Index to Advertisers